Vanessa Lockwood

REFLECTIONS OF LIFE

STRENGTH = ~~Stephanie~~
*****
WOMEN

The utmost Respect and Reverence; Just a Reminder, of who you are; I am proud my son chose you to be the mother of his children; this is the definition of Strength; Her name is a Lady; A good woman called ~~Steph~~;

Luv Ma II

To Stephanie: A Poem called STRENGTH
Steph

REFLECTIONS OF LIFE

STRENGTH! = Stephanie

by Vanessa Lockwood

Just to Remind you the Strength that comes from within; is the love that you carry in your heart; A strong woman; called the name of Steph; By a second Mother; who will always love you; No matter what; A good woman who deserves

RoseDog Books
PITTSBURGH, PENNSYLVANIA 15222

nothing but the best; the Mother of My grandson; who deserves
(over)

Jahovah stay with our women ~~Stephanie~~

Please guide her and protect her, Amen

All Rights Reserved
Copyright © 2004 by Vanessa Lockwood
No part of this book may be reproduced or transmitted
in any form or by any means, electronic or mechanical,
including photocopying, recording, or by any information
storage and retrieval system without permission in
writing from the author.

ISBN # 0-8059-9318-5
Printed in the United States of America

First Printing

For information or to order additional books, please write:
RoseDog Books
701 Smithfield St.
Pittsburgh, PA 15222
U.S.A.
1-800-834-1803
Or visit our web site and on-line bookstore at www.rosedogbookstore.com

THE TRANSFORMATION

As my boisterous eleven year old darted in the door, toward me Menna laid her knitting needles down to take in her son's eyes' Carl yelled, Mommy the mail, . . .

Oh dear Menna replied. What Have we here?

Casing the mail she stared in awe, there right on top was a letter From Anna. Anna whom she had not seen in almost twenty years, was arriving for her mothers' funeral in less than twenty four hours.

As I hurried myself through my housework routine, I Visualized Anna. Anna was ever so tiny, her height was about five Feet her jet black hair always glistened in the sun , pinned up in a Neat little croissant shaped roll, every hair was always in place. Her skin was the color of a caramel apple, smooth and soft, Anna Had eyes of a chocolate colored brown, which glistened in any light. Anna had to be about a size five, her legs shaped in the fashion of A baseball bat. Anna so small, but even so stately walked with "Head to the sky."

As I tried to sleep, I could not help but wonder to myself, the feel Of the letter from Anna felt troubling.

Oh you worry wart I told myself, considering Annas' reason for her visit I guess that would be troubling enough. Morning came and went with my usual routine. At about five o'Clock that evening the doorbell rang. "This better be good. I told myself".

I patted my head and tugged at my dress, took one last look at my two boys, as I gave them my warning eye and opened the door. EGAD! A feather could have knocked me over, who was this person?

Anna, I said, "yes, it's me in the flesh Anna replied", as I motioned her in I could not believe my eyes, Annas' face, I barely recognized, there was a Gray mist over her face hiding her natural beauty, her hair was pulled back In a ponytail, dry, brittle, with no luster. As I looked into her bloodshot eyes, the light was gone, her eyes looked like deep dark pools of nothingness, her stomach was swollen as if she was expecting, I bit my bottom lip to keep from asking her was she expecting.

As Anna sauntered pass me I caught a strong smell of alcohol As it whisked past me. As I introduced the boys, I noticed that Anna was extremely shaky, I immediately dismissed the boys.

As I sat down with Anna, I made it clear that I was there for her Anna Immediately burst into tears, as she opened up her purse and pulled out a burgundy flask. As Anna put the flask to her mouth I noticed the hunger with which she drank. As Anna began to relax, I said to her, "Anna what's' hurting you"? Are you so troubled, whereas life isn't worth living anymore? Anna, my little Anna let me help you.

Anna slowly looked up at me, Menna, said Anna, I have tried quitting for years, since my husbands violent death its been downhill all the way for me. I grabbed little Anna, hugged her, she was like putty in my hands, almost immediately, Anna passed out sleep.

I quietly put a blanket over Anna and thumbed through my phone book. I would call a friend of mine who will be able to help me get Anna into a treatment program, quickly; Mr. Perrone a long time friend rushed right over.

Well, it has been six months since Anna came to me. Anna who came to me a displaced person. The struggle still continues with Anna, I refuse to give up because I know something, I know at one time Anna was a credit and a beauty to the essence of the earth.

COUNT YOUR BLESSINGS

Staring at the calendar, counting off the days that my husband had been In the service, I asked myself? Why am I here?" He's been gone for ten months and yet it seems like an eternity. .

As I heard the loud crash coming from my two childrens playroom I quickly came back to earth, rushing to the childrens' playroom, I threw open the door, there they both were, covered in red and yellow finger paints, crouched down in the open closet with the clothing bar atop them.

Mark, Rachel, what on earth are you two doing? Three year old Rachel in her slippers and robe, stood up rubbing her eyes, pointing to her five year old brother Mark.

I went over examining the children to make sure that they weren't harmed, they were a little shaken up but otherwise fine. Children I hurriedly yelled let's have dinner, and dress for granma's house.

Mark started protesting, "I don't want to go to granmas' house she always pinches my cheeks, " Lets' go Mark , Menna said impatiently. Looking at Rachel, she just stood there with her finger in her mouth as if it didn't matter to Her one way or another, As I spooned broccoli onto the childens plates of burgers and fries, sat down and poured myself a cup of coffee, I thought to myself:

What a boring life, saddled down, married, with two children at twenty-one years old." Stop complaining, a voice said, "Mommy yelled Mark, Rachel is throwing french fries at me, "Mark finish your milk, granma will be here soon."

As I cleared the table the phone rang. "Hello dear this is your mother, calling to say that you should bring the kids to me, your fathers arthritis is acting up". "Yes ma we will be there shortly. Oh drats, replied Menna as She gently hung up the telephone. I grabbed Rachel in my arms and grabbed Marks' hand as we sauntered to the childrens' bedroom to get washed and dressed for granmas house, I sensed danger, something just was'nt right.

The children and me were making a game out of getting dressed, had I remembered to lock the door after I took the trash to the incinerator? I thought to myself, I had better check again, I glanced back at the children, Mark was tying Rachels' shoe.

Halfway to the door I realized that the door was ajar, "I thought to myself, that's funny", as I went to close and lock the door, the door burst open, catching me in the shoulder, I lost my balance and fell backwards. As I turned to get up, there inside my home was a crazed looking man, his six foot frame was standing directly In front of me, like a towering inferno, I looked up at his big wide open eyes. He had a cap pulled down over his forehead, so all I could see was those huge unfriendly eyes, he looked so angry, and his hands were huge.

I asked him, "Who are you? And what do you want?" as I prayed that the Children would remain quiet, my heart had to be pounding a mile a minute, this unkept stranger reached out and grabbed my right wrist, "I remembered the children, and I had to stay calm, to ensure their safety. He yanked me close to him, so that our bodies touched, I thought to myself "God please help me". Think fast; a voice said from out of nowhere, "I said to the stranger, "My husband only went to the store, he will be back shortly," AS HIS FREE-HAND depleted from his pocket.

TO BE CONTINUED...

Done with housework and the remainder of the laundry by 8 a.m., I ran the childrens' bath dressed and gave them a hot cereal breakfast. We headed out of the door by 10 a.m..Tess lived at the end of the hall, on passing her apartment, I noticed that the door was wide open, I heard the sound of the record spinning with the needle still intact on the record, However, no music came out Tess, I yelled, are you in there? NO answer, so I locked the door and continued on my way, "maybe she is at the laundromat downstairs, I said to myself, at either rate we have to get going.

First we went to visit the childrens' grandmother and grandfather, then we headed to the playground. After the children played for about forty –five minutes, I yelled "Is anybody hungry ? Mark and Rachel came running ready to eat lunch.

As the children sat eating, my thoughts went back to Tess, I glanced at my watch, it was 1:30 pm. I guess that worrying part of me began to take route. By 2:30 the children and me were in route home, we only lived across the street. Getting off the elevator I stared toward Tess' door, I didn't hear a sound, I said to myself, something must be wrong, my first Instinct was to bang on the door, but my mother instinct told me to take the children somewhere safe. I took my children to a neighbors house and hurried back to Tess; house. Menna yelled out Tess' name, no answer , I put my ear to the door, I heard the baby crying. I yelled "hang on Terry, I am going for help. I went to my apartment and phoned security. Security took thirty minutes to arrive. I explained the situation to the two officers, so they used a master key to open the door. The officers instructed me to wait outside, by that time I was frantic with worry,..The officers followed Terrys' cries, after checking each room for foul play. As I watched the officers make their way to Tess' room, my heart pounded', halfway to the room a dark tall figure lunged toward the officers, the officers subdued the intruder. I ran to Tess's room, on seeing , I could not tell if she was dead or alive, my heart almost stopped, "Oh God Tess, Tess, I started shaking her limp body", her face was beaten beyond recognition, her feet and hands were tied to the bed post, Little Terry was laying atop her mothers' lifeless body, yelling at the top of her lungs.

The police radioed for an ambulance, I ran over and grabbed Terry and took her out in the hallway. I took Terry to Mrs. Grace and phoned my mother and asked her to collect the children: after explaining the situation to her, I made my way back to Tess' "yes the officer nodded, she is still alive", oh Thank God, I said aloud.

Not much longer, I heard the roaring of sirens, I locked my door and checked the children, I told Mark to look after Terry and Rachel and wait for granma.

As, I climbed into the back of the ambulance, I held Tess' hand, she was beginning to come to, as I started to stare in disbelief at her battered body.

On arrival to the hospital I waited in the waiting room as Tess, was being examined by the doctor. The physician came out and informed me that Tess will make it, but she has been badly beaten and sustained multiple contusions, lacerations

Reflections of Life

Along with some hemorrhaging, she sustained a head injury, and there were traces of amphetamines in her blood stream, at least a five-day hospital stay. I was informed that I could visit with her. I went to Tess' room and told her what the doctor had said, Tess, I yelled, what is wrong with you, who was that creep, anyway? "Tess I guess you could say gets lonely without her fiancee, she relies heavily on men and good times". (Tess, good old gullible Tess), Tess looks at me, and replies, "just a guy".

Tess you fool you could have been killed, I yelled, (I am in tears by now) — I've got to get away from you, I'm not just going to stand back and watch you commit suicide, I started shaking her, trying to shake some sense into her head. Tess broke down into tears, and started apologizing, Tess how many times do I have to save you, you're always sorry but you never do anything about it, sorry, till you pick up the next bum and take him home,

Tess, in tears "please Menna don't do this, I'll change, I swear I'll change, what do you want me to do? Where is my baby.?. The kids are at my mothers house, and Tess, you won't get Terry unless you straighten out your life, Terry could have been killed, due to your negligence. Menna I'm sorry , please help me, what shall I do? Only please don't take Terry, Terry is all I have Tess why the men, Tess why? Tell me, I want to know the truth.

Okay! Shouted Tess", Jerry, Jerry left me. Menna...But the wedding plans the letter, I stammered.

Tess:..."Don't make me say it "he is already married, okay? Yelled Tess

Menna did a right about face, this news hit her like a ton of bricks, Tess, you could have come to me. Tess replied, I tried to tell you , but I just couldn't. Okay Tess, rest sweet Tess, just rest, I said consolingly to her, I will be back tomorrow, it is going to work out,. Tess you have to believe that, I kissed Tess on her forehead and left,. Tess handed me a spare key to her apartment, she winced in pain as she handed me the key.

I went home and just sat in the dark and thought, I asked God for strength.

Monday morning came, a plan had come to me throughout the night.

MY FIRST STOP WAS A VISIT TO Tess' house, As I stopped at Tess' door, I went inside with a spare key. While at Tess' house I picked up some things that she needed, robe, slippers, toothbrush etc., I packed her things neatly in an overnight bag, I grabbed Tess' black book, while picking up the book a feeling of fright came over me, that book is evil.

My thoughts went back to last night, when I couldn't sleep because of the traffic to and from Tess' house. That settles it, first stop to see the manager of the building. I explained to the manager about Tess and felt that she needed a transfer to a different building, or apartment, confidentially I added. The manager was very cooperative and agreed totally. As I left I thanked him, and started to the hospital. When I arrived at the hospital, Tess was sitting up, Menna briefed Tess on what I had done as far as the transfer. I asked Tess did she want to help herself and I informed her that she would have to move, and get away from that circle of friends, and start all over, building a new life for her and Terry. (Tess was so shaken up that she probably would have agreed to anything. handed Tess her black book, which she always carried with her, Tess stared at the book, wide eyed as she started to shake her head, Menna, take it, burn it, destroy it for me.

Menna put the book inside of her purse, Tess made me promise to destroy it, Menna said to herself. As I left the hospital, my mind centered on the book. There was a feel of fright in the air, and Menna knew that it was because of that black book. Menna had to get rid of that book, her heart was beating so fast, and her breathing felt irregular.

Menna went home and found a metal container, dropped the book inside the container and watched it burn, until I could see nothing but ashes, I started to feel like my old self again.

I dumped the ashes into the incinerator and said good riddance.

A funny thing about that black book, (the burning of that black book.),.The next day I went to see Tess, she still had some swelling, but her pimples were all gone, no trace of acne, she looked almost angelic in spite of it all, the light was back in her eyes, and I felt, a peaceful calm about her, almost as if a weight had been lifted from her. Tess nodded off to sleep, I watched a black cloud descend from her body and go out the door, I heard a voice say "everything is going to be alright", I looked and saw no one.

Tess' father died four months later, he left Tess a building. With a loan and a thirst for life, Tess opened the first battered womans' shelter in the area.

WHEN SILENCE IS NOT ALWAYS GOLDEN

Summer ending; time to go back to school and work, said Menna aloud; The children were excited about going back to school after a long tiring vacation.

Alright children said Menna , tomorrow is the big day, so lets' get back to our usual routine, which means bathtime; Ah; whined Rachel and Mark; I want to play with my dollies, said Rachel; Now Rachel, Mark, put your toys away lets' not give mommy a hard

REFLECTIONS OF LIFE

time; Okay replied the children in unison; (that was easy Menna thought).

As Menna bathed the children and dressed them for bed, by 9:00p.m., Menna said to herself (I wonder what this school year will bring)? Menna ,gently, tucked the children in after prayers and kissed them goodnight, Menna outened the light. "Mommy I'm thirsty , "cried Mark, me to said Rachel", okay kids said Menna, one drink and then off to sleep with you, however, when Menna returned with the childrens' water they were fast asleep.

As Menna sat on the sofa thumbing through her JC Penny' fall catalog, she prayed softly to herself. "Dear God please let this school year be a good one,. .Please don't let us lose any children, Now God you have' always helped me through, please help me this time; I feel a lot nervous about school, I don't know, maybe its' nothing.   AMEN

That morning the children and I walked to school; the children were happy to be going back to school; I wonder how long it would be before the novelty wore off, (Menna thought to herself).

On arrival to school , everything was chaotic; The police were there at school; As Menna found her way to the office, among the chaos, she noticed that the place was in a mess, like someone had lived here during the summer months; opened cans of unfinished food every where; candy wrappers, blankets, which were spread out as if someone had used them for bedding; What is going on, Menna asked Dr.Woods? It looks like someone might have lived here during the summer months; probably a displaced person, I don't think that it is serious, whoever it is is gone now.

Everyone pitched in for the cleanup, along with the Health Department, school is in session as usual kids.said Menna, as a group of the students and her climbed the stairs.

The Health Department was called in to investigate the incident; The Health Department supervised the clean-up.

As classes finally got underway; the day seemed to go along smoothly; that is until lunch, the kids were spilling things, getting into trouble for silly behavior problems ; There were about ten children who had to eat lunch in their homerooms for misbehaving.

After lunch myself, along with two monitors we went to collect the trays; The children' places were all cleaned, very good children; (Menna said to herself there is no evidence here that says the children even ate lunch),

Menna didn't think to much about it, I just went on with the day; That darn exit alarm keeps going off, I had better get security and find out what is going on. The childrens' behavior and that alarm continued for about two weeks.

One day Menna was walking past the library, when she heard voices behind the door; (On Monday the library was closed). Menna called maintenance for a spare key, maintenance came and opened the door. Menna noticed that there were children in the library playing, and the exit door was opened.

Children how did you get in here? Asked Menna, the door was locked. "The door was opened, replied Daniel. We just came in; "Boys get to class, said Menna; As the children held their heads down and went to class; Menna told maintenance, that there had been some strange occurrences going on here all this week, Russ the engineer agreed.

That night as Menna settled down after tending to the children, she thought about the days events; how on earth could children get behind a locked door?

Unless, someone opened the door from the inside. As Menna turned on the news, she noticed, staring at her posters of a boy and girl, who were missing; Kate Deveral age11, and Bradley Shaw, age 12; the children were last seen Wednesday, June 22; why that was the last day of school, Menna said to herself. The children left for school and and was neither seen or heard from since those dates.

My Menna said to herself; These are the same children who are on the milk carton; Well, said Menna I wonder if these two children are any relation to the stowaways who stayed in school this past summer.

Menna let the thought disintergrate from her mind. (Now Menna these are children, do you think that children can devise such a plan? Menna mumbled to herself. However. Mennas' voice told her, that children are a lot smarter and wiser these days, more so than we give them credit for.

Menna knew that she had an early morning ; so she thought it best for her to get to bed . Why, it is almost 2 am. As Menna noted the clock, Menna quickly jumped in bed, and outened the lights, only to be awakened by the clock alarm;

Rise and shine, Menna said to the children, as the children jumped up, without so much as a complaint, Menna thought , Maybe it will be a worthwhile day after all.

As, the children and Menna readied theirselves for school, they planned to drive, since the weather just wasn't warm anymore, this is September weather I guess. Mark and Rachel came running out of their rooms with all sorts of toys; "Children, where are you taking these toys, asked Menna". Rachel replied mommy, Mark has a secret; Rachel shhhh—-said Mark;

Okay kids said Menna, lets' leave the toys and get going.

On arrival to school there were fire trucks and smoke everywhere; There was a school fire in the back of the stage in the auditorium. It seemed that a hot plate was left plugged in an caused a fire, (Well our visitors are back, said Menna to herself).

Someone was here, said Dr Woods (the School Principal), now whoever it was is gone; Russ also reported his master keys missing, Dr. Woods, said Menna, I am beginning to think that the children know more than they are leading us to believe, We had better think about having a talk with the children tomorrow morning; Mrs Phillips said Dr. Woods, we are going to call the parents in today to pick the children up; Come tomorrow we will have everyone come to the auditorium, after the bell rings. The following morning the children all met in the auditorium, posters were passed out to the children and attending parents, the posters were of the two missing children,

Dr. Woods went on to tell the children, that these two children had been missing all Summer long, Dr. Woods, went on to say that these two children had been missing since the Summer and that their parents were worried sick, if you children know something , please write me a note and place it in the box on the stage of the auditorium, you do not have to leave your names. Parents' said Dr Woods, Children are to remain at home till further notice. I have been informed by the Board of Education, so that we can make sure that the school is safe, a thorough investigation will be conducted;. Children any notes, please drop them in the box before leaving the auditorium; children whose parents aren't here will remain in their seats until other arrangements can be made for a safe return home. Security was tight that day, teachers who want to volunteer their time to assist authorities in the investigation are welcome. After Dr. Woods and I went over a list of occurrences, we figured that whoever the intruder was the children knew and trusted this person or persons; Also the length of time that those two children had been missing pointed to when our problems here at school, started. We alerted the staff as to our findings, and told them to be on guard, this intruder is coming and going at will, we must be careful.

The following day, unmarked cars were posted outside at all the school exits, waiting and watching.

That night Mark wanted to make his weekly visit to the bank to put his $5:00 in his savings account, Menna watched Mark go into the room and lift up the hatch in his bedroom ceiling, where his secret hiding place was. That secret hatch kept flashing through Mennas' mind, there is one just like that in the cafeteria at school; Reject supplies are kept there, no one hardly ever goes up there; Ouch, something pinched Menna, really hard.

Menna called Dr. Woods at school that Thursday and told hew what had happened. "Dr. Woods, replied, you know Mrs. Phillips, I thought about that, no one even knows it is there, except for about one or two staff members, yo u have to study the blueprints to find it, will you be in today? Mrs Phillips? Asked Dr. Woods? (Yes replied Menna, I would like to look into this with you, we"" had better let the authorities handle this, said Dr. Woods, we don't know what to expect.

After taking the children to their grandparents for the day, Menna went to school, investigators were there along with Dr. Woods. As we made our way up to the top floor; following' investigators; my heart was pounding (Menna), felt another pinch, ouch said Menna, are you alright said Dr. Woods? Yes, replied Menna. As investigators opened the hatch and climbed into the ceiling; Dr. Woods and Menna waited nervously. As they stood there looking up, out came two of the investigators, one was holding his arms up as if waiting to be handed something . We watched them lower the two children from that ceiling panel, a boy and a girl, these are the missing children, Menna and Dr. Woods repeated the same thought at the same time, Dr. Woods' and Menna stared at each other in disbelief.

As we watched the authorities take the children down to the nurses office, to be examined by one of their doctors, we looked at the children, and the pictures of the children, those children were at least ten pounds heavier than their pictures.

The children were tired. They kept saying that they wanted to go home; Children, said Dr. Woods, how did you get here ? Whose idea was this? Apparently the children had taken up shelter in the school with some help from some of our students. can you believe that the children were feeding and clothing these children. The childrens' parents were notified, the children were fine, had gained a little weight, needed a bath. But otherwise were fine.

Children play a very crucial role in our lives, they suffer because to hurt a child, you are tampering with the ultimate gift from God. It is our responsibility to protect our children.

The Earth Has Eyes

Can you recognize life as the way it should be?
Then open your eyes and see;
The children who have not yet been found;
This is serious, because God wears a frown.

The sufferage and pain is to much to bear;
When a child cries out and no one is there;

Pain, fear, and death, still to be carried out;
Until the gift of love ., No longer is locked out.

REFLECTIONS OF LIFE

As I reached the eighth floor, out of breath, I ran the length of the hallway, through the trap door, I approached the exit door with caution, panting and gasping for air, "Melody you have the most wonderful gift. Melody you have the gift of life. What you put into it you get out of it, but Melody, you have got to try, life comes with no guarantees, "Melody, please live.

Melody -- Menna at this point, I choose not to live, I feel as if I am on a roller coaster going nowhere.

Menna: Melody, what about those lives you have touched, doesn't that even matter to you? The pain, the grief, that you will be sending your parents through, your gift Melody,. Your gift of life, your daughter. There are countless others Melody. Melody there is more... please hear me out, Menna said, as she walked toward, Melody, began to inch closer and closer to the ledge. Melody please, please listen, the drugs are affecting you, let me take you to a place where they can help you, we love you Melody, please live don't do this. Hearing a crowd gathering below yelling no, don't do it, I saw Melody sway backward and forwards like a moving pendulum. I lunged for Melody, and tackled her , Melody yelled NO! fought me, we rolled along the perimeter of the area of the roof. Melody listen to me, (I yelled, so out of breath) I can't let you do this.

Melody yelled, let me go, I was on top of her putting the weight of my knees down on her shoulders. Melody was hysterical, yelling, let me go, mind your own business.

Melody, Menna said Tears clouding her eyes "It is my business, your life is my business. Melody calmed down, yelling, okay, okay, just let me up. I was out of breath, breathing heavily as I released my weight off her shoulders.

Almost instantly, Melody was up yelling, Menna "please forgive me. It is easier for me this way, (Melody stop, I'm tired, I cannot do this, Menna yelled.

Menna ran towards Melody, grabbing for anything, as she jumped off the ledge. Menna managed to grab her wrist. (It was almost as if Melody was being given a second chance to change her mind, this wasn"t' suppose to happen).

Menna let me go, I don't want to live yelled Melody. Melody I can't hold on, please help me, please live; Melody opened the hand of her subdued wrist, wide, wider, widest, Melody was slipping.

That day I watched Melody fall fifteen stories down to her death; I sat there on that roof top, I don't know how long; I was weak, drained, hurt, and angry; I saw the signs, but I looked the other way, I looked the other way because it hurt to bad. I did what most people do, I tried to spare me, I didn't think about Melody or her pain, or what she was going through.

I felt close to God up there that high, I looked up at the stars and I said God, Please hear me, does anybody care? Oh God why does it have to be this way, why can't everybody be happy, why is happiness something that we have to earn? Why couldn't Melody had lived? Why did she have to die, why did she have to take drugs. I sat there, I couldn't move I felt frozen. I saw lights flashing, And I heard voices, different voices, coming from here and coming from there, I don't remember much after that, I remember waking up to the antiseptic smell of the hospital, I remember my mom and dad staring down lovingly at me, I remember asking God to tell me what to do, I can't let Melody, just die, I have to do something, God tell me what to do, Melody, her life, was worth something, God, tell me what to do, please don't let Melody die in vain.!

MELODY—-my dear sweet Melody

I watched you bloom, But when you started to
Wither, I did nothing.
Melody—I wonder what life will bring with out
You? More deaths, more grief, more lost souls,
That still remain.

Melody—to me you are special, to me you are
Somebody, to me, I feel that you are alive in so many.

My dear sweet Melody, will you rest in peace
As flowers bloom atop you in a rainbow of colors,
I think to myself, this is the beauty of Melody.
This much beauty in death does she bring.
Just a preview of the beauty her life could have obtained.

GOD THERE ARE TOO MANY OF US DYING

REFLECTIONS IN LIFE ...   A SECOND CHANCE

Starring nervously at the clock, realizing that the boys and myself were running late, I quickly cleared the breakfast dishes and

REFLECTIONS OF LIFE

instructed the children to get there needed textbooks for school.

Thank goodness my job was at the same school that my children attended, we would be about fifteen minutes late. It was a nice day, we had planned to walk, but considering the time, we took the car, the children started protesting, they preferred to walk. They wanted to see Luther. Luther was an old stray cat who always walked to school and home with the children, who had made his home up under our house. The children kept feeding him so Luther wasn't about to leave.

The children named him Luther, because it was on the birthday of Dr, Martin Luther King that Luther came to us. I looked at it being a blessing in disguise, since that day there was no school, the children were bored, and very testy. When out of the blue we heard purring coming from the side of the house, with a flashlight in hand we went to investigate, and found a beautiful brown chestnut kitten who later became known as Luther. We had to keep Luther out doors because the children had a dog named "Mohammad", now a full grown pit bull, who didn't take kindly to Luther.

When the weather turned cold we made arrangements with our next door neighbor to keep Luther, however, when summer rolls around, for the past two years, Luther has slept under the house, and sometimes at our neighbors. Our neighbor is kind , to let the children visit with Luther, anytime they please.

"Children, I replied above their protests, I promise you tomorrow we will see Luther. The children didn't want to give in, but I guess they noticed the urgency in my voice, so they agreed".

As I pulled into the school parking lot, I looked at my watch "just as I predicted (15 mins. Late). As Menna signed in checking her mailbox, she had a copy of new student transfer sheets, One name stuck in her head "Melanie Rodgers, no it couldn't be. As I entered the office, I yelled good morning everyone shouted (good morning) in unison, I knocked on the principals inner office door, "I had to find out about Melanie Rodgers," (come in a voice called out), Menna went in.

Doctor Woods, was a young woman, very concerned and caring, really a dedicated woman. Mrs. Woods, is there anything that you can tell me about a new student, named "Melanie Rodgers"?

Its' a long story Dr. Woods, said Menna, do you have a few minutes? I have about ten minutes Mrs.. Phillips, replied Dr. Woods. As I began to tell Dr. Woods that story, she was deeply moved. Mrs. Phillips I don't think it wise for you to delve into this, Dr, Woods, When Melody died, it just left me feeling so empty inside, I have not yet been able to fill that emptiness. I don't know what I am grasping at, I only know that somehow, I feel that I owe Melody something, "Mrs. Phillips, replied Dr. Woods, check with me after dismissal, let us see what we can come up with. Mrs. Phillips if this is your Melanie, you have to let her come to you. I urge you, to approach this situation whatever it may be, with tact, and caution, is that understood? "yes ,Dr. Woods", I replied. Also Dr. Woods, went on to say" your PTA\ Board meeting has been rescheduled, the superintendent was called to Albany, the computers that the PTA purchased has arrived, and , the auditorium will be free the twenty-second of February for your plant sale, (I was a PTA Board Member—(Menna).

Now Mrs. Phillips, putting all business aside, you and I have been friends for a very long time, so from one friend to another, good luck, Menna. (Thank you Sandy, Menna replied).

As Menna rose to leave, she could hardly wait for dismissal. Seeing Melanie sitting in my class, her big brown eyes, looking up at the blackboard she reminded me of her mother (Melody) all over again, The bell rang, after dismissal I checked my mail box and took my mail home,

On arrival home, I sat the children at the kitchen table to do their homework and proceeded to go over the mail from school. Bingo! Screamed Menna, this young lady was Melody's daughter. Melanie was fifteen years old, and living with her grandparents; Melanie was listed in that coming from a troubled family, category, branded a troubled teen, but could be saved with that needed push.

At that moment Mark let out a piercing scream, "what is your problem Marcus, Menna asked, (Rachel kicked me, whined Mark); Rachel, sit next to me and let me see , what you have done with your homework situation. Menna checked Rachels' homework and reviewed it with her. Your turn Mark, Mark handed Menna his homework paper, I checked it and we went over it together. After homework the children and Menna watched the afterschool special, and ate dinner. By 9:00p.m. Menna had the children in bed and bathed. They were tired since they had been up since 6:30 am that morning, They didn't protest, just drifted off to sleep.

On arriving to school the next day, after checking attendance, I noticed that Melanie was not in school, I went up to the office and phoned her grandparents, I arranged to go after school. I took Mark and Rachel to their grandparents before meeting with Melanies' grandparents. finally Menna arrived at Mr and Mrs. Rodgers house (Menna arrived_);

Melanies' grandparents, recognized Menna,; Menna let them know that it was a pleasure seeing them again.

Menna explained to them her concerns regarding Melanie, pertaining to her frequent absentees, and Melanies' withdrawal from her classmates; (Melanie) seemed so withdrawn most of the time. How is Melanie here at home? Mrs Rodgers bit her lip, and told me that she did not know what had gotten into Melanie, these last couple of years, she somehow got herself mixed up with the wrong crowd. Melanie, doesn't listen to a word we say, Melanie does, just what Melanie wants to do.

I asked the Rodgers, were drugs involved? Mrs. Rodgers, everytime the phone rings, I get that eerie feeling that something terrible has happened. Menna rose to leave, thanking the Rodgers for their time. Menna left her phone number with the Rodgers, and asked them to call if Melanie showed up.

On Mennas' drive home she stopped to see her two scouts, (these two teenage boys often helped Menna in situations such as this, they knew the kids in the area and where to find them. Menna paid the two boys twenty dollars each, every week as long as they attended school and did their homework, Menna also tutored the boys on the weekend. The boys were model high school students.

There parents were in law enforcement, so I guess those skills and know how rubbed off on them. That morning before leaving for work and school, the boys called me with an address where Melanie spent a lot of days and nights, I was informed that she rarely stayed home, Menna thanked her scouts and went off to work. After dismissal the children and I went home and had a snack, did our homework, and chatted about various things, before I realized it, it was dinner time. We ate dinner, watched a program, bathed, showered and were in bed by 9:30. That night the phone woke Menna up, I looked at the clock, "Oh my goodness, Said Menna, it is 4:a.m..

On answering the phone Menna recognized the voice of her elder scout. "Hello Mrs Phillips, this is king tut (code name), "Where are you Menna asked., at home now he replied, What is it ;asked Menna ? Its' Melanie, she's in trouble, she needs help." I am on my way Menna replied.

Menna banged on Ms. Clarks door, she answered sleepily. Ms. Clark please sit with the children, a child is in trouble, I have got to go, "What else is new Menna, you hurry yourself along. I'm on my way. Ms. Clark was my next door neighbor who was familiar with my late night and morning emergencies), she always made herself available.

A SECRET PLACE

On arriving to school and work that morning, I noticed the hecticity of the office staff; What is going on Dr. Woods asked Menna, oh it is little Thomas, he's been missing since last Friday, his parents phoned to see if the school has had any contact with him.

What happened, I asked? Thomas was grounded for a behavior problem since last Thursday, now this Friday little Thomas decides to run away from home. Ms. Woods I think I might know where Thomas is. There is a place, which he calls his secret place. Anything that you can come up with Mrs. Phillips would be a great help.

Menna drove that winding road to a secret place; Menna thought about inquisitive little Thomas, always asking questions, so studious, so precise.

Menna finally reached the abandoned rail car yard, Menna blew the horn and waited for a response, there was none. In the distance Menna heard the4 faint barking of a dog, as Menna walked the length of the track towards an old abandoned caboose, Menna saw Topper, (Thomas' dog), wagging his tail trying to get me to follow him, as Menna followed Topper , Topper led Menna to little Thomas.

Little Thomas had fallen from the abandoned caboose and hit his head on something, he looked to be unconscious. I ran to the car and grabbed two blankets, phoned for an ambulance on the car phone, and headed back to Little Thomas. I wrapped blankets around Little Thomas, and waited for the ambulance to arrive. Menna, dared not move him.

Finally the ambulance arrived, as Menna waved them down, Menna watched the paramedics rush over to her, via stretcher. As they knelt over Thomas. They asked me if I was a relative, Menna replied., he is one of my students, I will notify his parents if I ca n have some information, as to what hospital he will be going to and what is the extent of his injury.

The paramedic replied "well lets see, his name please," his name is Thomas Miller, Thomas is twelve years old, a student at West Central Elementary School, I am one of his teachers, Mrs Phillips.

"Well Mrs. Phillips, replied the paramedic, Thomas has a head injury, the extent of the injury has not yet been determined, Thomas has a couple of cracked ribs, these injuries are at least seventy-two hours old. We will be enroute to the Childrens' Hospital, please ask the parents to meet us there.

On arrival to the hospital Menna recognized Thomas' parents, they rushed over to me as I ushered them to the clerk we were directed to the waiting room. The doctor walked hastily over to the Millers, telling them that Thomas, had sustained a serious head injury, and a fractured right arm. The doctor stated that Thomas would be under observation for at least seventy-two hours. After that time it will be determined when he would be released, we were allowed to visit.

I thought to myself " I had better get back to my own children, replied Menna to herself, as she started to leave. Menna reassured the Millers that everything would be alright , they thanked Menna and Menna went to her car.

Thoughts of my children flashed through my mind, I felt that my children deserved a big treat for being so understanding, I looked at my watch, it was 2:00p,m, (A whole day gone), Menna knew just what kind of treat it would be.. As Menna pulled into the school yard, signed out, and went to collect the children, Menna noticed, that Mark had a look of disappointment on on his face, He hadn't seen me that day and probably fretted, I forgot to inform the kids before I left the building.

As the children and I climbed in the car, I said children, close your eyes and don't peek, I have a surprise, Menna saw Marks' face light up. Oh good I thought, Rachel just sat there playing with her stick-ons, Close your eyes Rachel, Rachel complained, "do I have to: I want to play, "Rachel stop being a spoiled sport, we're almost there.

Rachel closed her eyes and we pulled into the big McDonalds' parking lot, It was the childrens' favorite one since they had Ronald McDonald there in person, playing with the children at the Mc Donalds Playground.

Open your eyes kids, the children opened their eyes and squealed with excitement, as they played, Menna ordered their favorite Happy Meals, and asked if if she could have them in one half hour, that way the children would have enough time to play with Ronald Mc Donald.

After the children ate, I said, okay children one more surprise, close your eyes, we drove to the Cinema Movie House, there was a new Ninja Turtle Movie that the kids were just dying to see.

As I pulled into the parking lot, I told the children to open their eyes, "Surprise, Menna said , as we raced to the ticket booth, Rachel said' "mommy we ,still have homework. "No you don't said Menna, this is our no homework day, we will do our homework tomorrow."

The children were asleep before we even made it home; I looked over at them and they both had smiles on their faces.

Well, I guess that alls' well that ends well.

THE STRANGER

She came running through the emergency room door, as she ran through the opened door, her head hit the side of the open door (Blam), the sound startled me. She was screaming and crying at the same time, she ran right past me to the examining room, it was there she collapsed,

The staff ran over to her immediately. I called a code ten, as I notified the operator, I noticed the door of the emergency room was covered in blood, where her head hit. As I went to pick up the phone to notify the police, a man came up behind me, sat down calmly, quietly drew out his gun, and cautioned me not to call the police.

I laid the phone down quietly, asked the gentlemen, what had happened. He replied, it was an accident, sweating, shaking, I only wanted to scare her not to shoot her. He broke down into tears, it just went off.

I said please give me the gun, as he reached over to hand me the gun, I said, who is this woman to you ? She is my fiancee, we were going to be married, he sobbed.

Sir please let me help you, let me notify the proper authorities, who are better equipped at handling such things.

Is she going to be alright, he asked, sir I don't know, I have to check, but before I do, I need to know if you are going to do the right thing? You have to let me notify the police, will you do that? She was a lady of the night, I followed her, I watched her, she said she loved me, we were going to be married, how could she do this to me, he sighed.

Sir, sometimes things that happen in our lives don't seem fair, but its' life, the way it is today. We have to take what life has to offer us, and that means taking the bitter with the sweet, and if it makes us unhappy then it is up to us to make a change.

"I guess my life is over", he replied. Sir, it is not over until God says that it is over. We all make mistakes, sometimes serious , sometimes not so serious, but that is because we are imperfect human beings, we have consequences that we must withstand. It is up to you to take that step toward manhood, you have to turn yourself in, you have to take responsibility for this, only then can you have a second chance.

There exists happiness, you have to find it and hold on tight, it doesn't have to be this way. Sir, so what do you want me to do. (his reply), how is she? (I knew that the young woman had died, but I just didn't know if I should tell this distraught man, now , at this time, "you have got to tell, let it be his choice to either stay, or walk away" (a voice said).

Sir, I am going to tell you that your fiancee, she didn't make it, I'm sorry.

The gentleman jumped up and started to pace the floor, his whole body was shaking,. Sir, it is your choice, I can notify the police and you can stay, or I can notify the police and you can walk out, before you say anything, remember ""It is up to you to set yourself free". The stranger stood up and walked out. The funny thing is, is that fear did not take over, I wasn't afraid.

MENNA called the police, when the police arrived Menna told them what she knew and handed them the gun.

While the police were still in my office, I happened to see the stranger, he was on the monitor coming in the side entrance. As he neared the emergency waiting room area, I held my breath,

The stranger walked over to me and said thank you. He turned towards the police, arms outstretched, the handcuffs went on and out they walked.

WISDOM

Looking at my dad, as he wears
His crown of glory;
I can't help but think, he must've
Been a warrior.

Looking at my dad, and the knowledge
In his eyes; always knowing my troubles,
My woes, my pains, my fears;

Not uttering a word, but always
Responding to my woes, with that
Something wonderful that only dad
Can know.

A dad is a wonderful thing, standing
With his head so high;
Looking as if any moment he'll
Skyrocket to the sky.

IN LOVING MEMORY OF MY DAD

THE GLASS HOUSE
(In Loving Memory of Our Fathers Against Violence)

On my arrival home from school I walked to the door of our home, As I put my key inside the door I could smell the fresh baked goods sneaking under the door.

I let myself in, went over to my mom (who was in the kitchen baking for her church baked good sale, and preparing spaghetti and spicy meatballs, "a recipe of hers".

As I looked at the back of my mothers' small frame, I started to realize how dear she really was Mom had her hair fixed up in a neat little bun. Her perfume had a scent of lemons, my mother turned to me, as I noticed her brown sparkley eyes; her cinnamon complexioned skin tone; her high cheek bones, which accented her wide smile, mom replied "Good Afternoon".

MENNA walked over and kissed her mom, as she rummaged through the refrigerator for the milk, mom said, "Menna you have several phone messages, you are late today, why is this may I ask? WE had a student council meeting, said Menna, we are trying to come up with a band for the weekend. Hopefully we will be able to find three different groups,that everybody likes ,that we can use year round. That way it will make things a lot easier.

My, replied mom , you sure are busy for a sophomore. "It helps mother I answered". Kissing her soft cheek, I quickly grabbed a cupcake and a and a glass of milk and went to my room, loaded down with books as usual. As I grabbed my phone messages (Menna), I noticed that, there were three, but the message from Ebony is the one that stuck in my mind.

Menna thought about Ebony, we attended the same school, Ebony was fuller figured than most of us.

Ebony had sandy brown hair, with hazel eyes. Her mother was killed in a car accident many years ago, her father was her legal guardian.

Ebony was always so quiet, rarely smiled, and didn't get involved in the school activities or with friends. I guess that's why I thought it strange that she should call, since you rarely saw ebony, only at school. She took that bus ride with us but as far as conversation from everybody else.

Well maybe I will give Ebony a call before hitting the books.

Menna picked up the phone and dialed Ebony. A male voice on the phone gave me the third degree; "Who is this.? Where do you know Ebony from? Hold on.

As Ebony came to the phone, I could hear someone pick up the extension hello Ebony I said, I called to see if you would like to attend the school dance with a group of us this Friday, we will be home by twelve, most of the guys will be meeting us there. I don't know replied Ebony nervously, I will let you know in school tomorrow. Okay Ebony, I will see you then. As Menna hung up the phone, a shudder went through her, why was Ebony so shaky all the time, oh well, I will see her in school tomorrow. I did not see Ebony nor did I see her in school that day. Menna decided to pay Ebony a visit after the game.

As the dismissal bell rang, I thought to myself "thank goodness," I gathered up my books. MENNA stopped at the pay phone to call her mother and inform her that she would be late, the basketball game is after school, Menna said to her mother (Mrs Brown).

I would like to stop and see Ebony after the game, she was not in school today.

Okay dear mom replied, I will put dinner into the warmer, Okay mom see you later on.

The game was a good one, Turner Carrol beat Cardinal O'Hara by six points. We didn't cheer any specific team since the private high schools were not male and female integrated as of yet, We wanted the boys to patronize our dances. On arriving to Ebonys' house, Menna rang the bell, and knocked on the door, I heard voices shouting at each other, but no one came to the door, so Menna left.

When Menna arrived home there was a message on her answering machine that Ebony had phones, Menna called Ebony immediately.

As Ebony picked up the phone and said hello, I asked her why wasn't she in school today? "Oh I had a doctors' appointment Ebony replied, How about the dance will you be attending, Sure replied Ebony, We are all going with Donna since she has a car pick you up at seven.

Ebony phoned me three times that Friday, I am going to the dance, I am not going to the dance, finally I am going to the dance.

As the music reached a feverish pitch, I said excuse me, (I needed some air),

When Menna went outside she noticed that Ebonys' father was parked out front in his car.

MENNA: didn't think anything of it, she just went and told Ebony that her dad was out front. Ebony started shaking and ran to the ladies room yelling "tell him you cannot find me". Menna informed the ushers, that Ebony didn't want to be found, Well what shall we do replied the ushers? Let, Sister Mary Peter handle it. Good idea, replied Dan, the elder usher.

As we informed Sister Mary Peter' as to what was going on, she immediately met Ebony's dad at the door.

Mr. Tollidge finally left, and Sister Mary Peter motioned me to her office. As we went to Sister Mary Peters' office, I wondered what is this all about?

As we went to Sister Mary Peter' office, I wondered what is this all about? Sister Mary Peter sat down at her desk, and asked me how well did I know Ebony, Menna replied "we are casual acquaintances, Ebony is a recluse, no one has ever visited Ebony inside her home.

See if you can get Ebony to open up to you, if there is a problem, tell Ebony that she can come to me.

Yes sister replied Menna; "What am I looking for., Menna asked: I don't know, replied Sister Mary Peter, it is just a feeling that I have. As Menna left the office she shook her head, saying to herself "grownups are strange. Menna went back to the auditorium, she informed Ebony that her dad had left he seemed upset about something, Menna said to Ebony, What did you do?

Ebony did not say anything, We all loaded into the car and headed to Als' for burgers and shakes, before going home. When Menna arrived home, mom had left out milk and cookies for her, with a note which read, lets' talk tomorrow at 7:00p.m. see you then. LOVE MOM.

Menna showered,and went to bed, I (Menna), was asleep by 12:30. The phone rang, it woke Menna up abruptly. Menna looked at the clock, "great, said Menna, 2:00 AM. Hello Menna sleepily said as she answered the phone. Menna, can I come there now, I have to get away, he is going to kill me, "Who replied Menna", I cannot talk now, just let me in, "Okay, replied Menna.

Menna hung up the phone, and reached for her robe, Menna went into mommas' room to let her know what had just happened. Menna gently closed her mothers' bedroom door, and went to the kitchen and turned on the tea kettle. Menna sat at the table and thought to herself, what is wrong with Ebony? Am I prepare for this? Menna answered herself, "so I don't know, but Ebony, needs someone."

As the tea kettle whistled loudly, Menna got up to prepare the tea, Menna heard someone say "Menna , whatever it may be, please remain calm and subdued, don't let shock show on your face, you can do it". "Okay, replied Menna", Menna looked back and as usual there was no one there.

Menna finally sat down to her tea, when, she heard a loud banging on the door. Menna immediately, hurried to the door, Menna looked through the peep- hole, and saw Ebony hysterically crying. Menna opened the door, and Ebony ran in gasping for air, crying uncontrollably. As Ebony ran to me, I thought she would knock me down. Menna put her arms out and Ebony ran right into them.

Ebony, dear God what on earth is the matter, "Ebony blurted out, he beat me and made me have sex with him", (her eyes, blackened and closed). Who beat you? Asked Menna, who made you have sex with them. "Him, replied Ebony, my father. Oh God Ebony, I am sorry, said Menna. Ebony please calm down, you're alive, you're here.

Menna poured Ebony a cup of tea, and sat on the sofa alongside her, I said "its' going to be alright", here drink this tea, and maybe a hot shower and you will be as good as new, you had better get some sleep, we can deal with this better in the morning. Menna, said Ebony, "I am carrying his child. Oh God, thought Menna, she is going to need a doctor, I had better get momma, Ebony, wait here, Menna locked the door and ran to her mommas' room, after informing her mother, her only reply was "poor child", hand me my phone book, Menna, I am going to call Eloise with child services before I see Ebony, she can get a doctor here quicker than I can. (Momma was a retired social worker).

Momma made a phone call and ushered me out of the room, later she joined

Ebony and me in the family room. Now Ebony, I have called a nice young lady over who can help you, you are not to go home, Wait here for her. Is that understood. "yes mam Ebony replied". Moments later their was a banging at the door, momma looked out through the peep-hole, only to see Ebony's father, he was swearing, and yelling for Ebony to come out. Momma said, "Menna take Ebony to the back of the house". Momma ran to the closet and pulled out her shotgun, she never o pened the door.

Momma yelled, Ross, Ebony is here with me, the police are on the way, you go home Ross and wait for notification. Ross yelled "Ebony is my daughter, she does what I tell her to do", as he kicked and punched at the door, Momma replied, now Ross, I have a loaded shot gun here , pointed at you, (momma pointed the shotgun directly at the peephole). Now Ross I thank you kindly to leave the premises or I will shoot you, said momma. Momma pointed the gun up towards the corner of the kitchen , and fired, now Ross, said momma what is it going to be? Ebony's dad yelled, I will be back old woman, don't think that you have gotten rid of me that easy, he finally left, momma leaned up against the door and took a deep breath.

Not long after that Eloise arrived, "she explained to Ebony that she was going to take her with her to a safe place and to see a doctor. Ebony, don't worry everything is going to be okay for you.

Eloise spoke to Ebony " Ebony, where I am taking you, you are not alone,. There are others just like you, you can have the baby and then later give the baby up for adoption, there is a school you can attend with girls in similar situations, you will be safe, and you will have people to talk to about this traumatizing experience. Are you ready? " Yes, Ebony replied, but my dad, "Eloise cut Ebony off", now don't you worry about him. We will wait for the police to arrive and then we will be on our way.

Mrs. Eloise Banks: will you be informing the school about Ebonys' whereabouts, one of the nuns' Sister Mary Peter has been concerned about Ebony. Mrs. Banks assured momma and me that would be all taken care of.

The police finally arrived, and as Ebony and Mrs. Banks left I silently prayed "God please be with Ebony, please guide, direct , and protect her, God please keep her close to your heart, I know there is no protection greater than yours. God please, just this one last favor.   AMEN

GOD I ALWAYS SAY THAT, IT IS NOT REALLY MY LAST FAVOR; AMEN.

ell I haven't heard from Ebony, but I know that she is safe, Eloise reassured me. I know that Ebony, graduated high school and is now attending college.

Last night I dreamed that Ebony was serving dinner to two children, and I saw a kindly man sitting at the head of the dinner table reading the paper. Ebony was smiling , as she sat down at the beautiful dinner table. Menna saw Ebony and th kindly looking man along with two children, bow their heads a give thanks.

As Menna saw herself nearing what looked like a stop sign she took care to read, the sign read the end. Maybe I will never hear from Ebony again, sometimes things happen in our lives and we often time like to leave the bad memories behind, that's alright I guess.

But, I am thankful that God took the time to let me know that Ebony was alright. As for Ebonys' dad well he was never seen or heard from again, a group of fathers in our area has a club entitled MEN AGAINST VIOLENCE.

These fathers got together and paid Mr. Ross a visit, anyway the next thing I knew he was gone, packed and gone. I guess that is one of the good things that came out of this, "The Fathers' Against Violence", now when we children are faced with a dilemma, we can go to the fathers' whose headquarters is in the complex. NOW WE ARE REALLY ONE BIG HAPPY FAMILY.

THE END, WE LOVE YOU DADS.

HEAVEN HELP US ALL!

Oh that darn itching, Menna squealed as she lay in bed unable to sleep. I think that the children and myself will take a ride to the Mall tomorrow after work, maybe I will go to that new soap shop, "Soaps and More", said Menna; maybe it is my soap that is causing the problem. Menna must have tossed and turned all night. The clock alarm finally went off and up Menna popped, as Menna looked over beside her for her husband, David, Menna reminded herself, oh that's' right, David is at the base.

It is 6:30 am, said Menna, I think I will have a quick cup of coffee before waking the children. Okay children Menna said at 7:00am rise and shine, the children sleepily dragged themselves out of bed; Menna quickly cleaned and dressed her children, Menna sat the children down to a breakfast of cream of wheat, pastry, milk and juice; Menna showered and moisturized, slipped on her robe and cleared the breakfast dishes and sat the children down to watch the Discovery Channel. There was a special on animals, the children loved animals, Menna finally dressed herself for work.

Kids time to go yelled Menna, from her bedroom, get your books and lunches, "Mommy when is daddy coming home asked Rachel? Daddy will be home the weekend, replied Menna. The children and Menna walked that warm day with Luther trailing them. (Luther was the childrens' stray cat, who followed them to and from school).

Work was a long and tiring day. I guess it was the heat. The day finally over it was time to pack it in and go home. As the children and Menna walked home to pick up the car, Menna told them that we were going to the mall. How would you like to go to the game room; I could hear the excitement in their voices, as the children yelled, yea—-.

As Menna looked up at an overhead tree and noticed countless bees, Menna quietly closed and locked the car doors. Off Menna and the children went to the Mall, playing their count the cars game. (We all picked our favorite color, and counted our color car, whoever had the most cars of their color at the end of the trip, won a free scoop of ice cream. Menna always lost, since she had to watch the road

On arrival to the mall, Menna and the children went into the soaps and more shop. Menna found some fruit scented fragrances, which were hypo-allergenic. That store brought Menna into a deep depression, just all of a sudden. Menna hurriedly made her purchase and Menna and the children left the store. Menna still did not feel comfortable, she felt an uneasiness about something. (What is it now? Menna said to herself).

The children enjoyed the video arcade (game room). We ordered pizza and soft drinks there afterwards. On arrival home, the children and Menna did their usual homework, watched the after school special, and played old maid. The children were in bed asleep by 8:30p.m. Menna ran her milk bath and tried out the new soap. Menna did not itch, but that depression did not lift. Menna drifted off to sleep at about midnight. At about 4:00a.m. Menna was awakened by what seemed to be babies crying out; Menna looked out her bedroom window, There on Mennas' roof was at least twenty cats, including Luther, Menna hurriedly closed her bedroom window as Luther jumped into Mennas' bedroom window.

That was terribly frightening said Menna, I wonder what brought that on. Menna layed back down and tried to sleep. Well at least we do not have to wake up to any alarms in the morning, thought Menna, tomorrow was Saturday.

Menna was awakened that morning by something in her bed; Menna jumped up and pulled the covers back; (My God said Menna), There were at least fifty dead bees and wasps in Mennas' bed, As Menna looked out of her bedroom window, right in her right hand upper corner of her room window was what looked like a hive or a bees nest, it was covered with wasps and bees, Menna did not even know that bees and wasps nested together like that.

Mennas, neighbor came over and climbed out on the roof with a can of raid and knocked the nest down.

David finally arrived home and Menna could not help but wonder the reason for those two incidents, just what did it mean? Menna must have pondered on that idea off and on all day. That Friday the children and my husband drove to the Waterfront park for frozen yogurt, before he went to work on the base that day. Menna had planned a barbecue for the children and herself that afternoon; Menna looked at her watch, it was a little after 3:00p,m, as Menna, David and the children silently drove home, Menna was deep in thought about these incidents.

Honey, said Menna, aren't you due on the base by 4:00p.m.; You got it babe, replied David, it is about a 45 minute drive, we are making good time..

As we pulled into the driveway, Menna said honey about last night, the cats; David kissed Menna full on the mouth and said, dear we will discuss it when I get home tonite, Bye daddy squealed the children as David pulled off for work; honk, honk; David blew his horn as we watched him drive out of our sight.

Okay kids, time for a barbecue; the children helped Menna set up; Mommy can we play our new video game asked Mark; Sure kids lets' go get set up and I will cook and you play, Menna finally got the children settled and went back to cookout business; Menna made sure monitors were on first.

While grilling, Menna was facing away from the grass, when Menna turned to go indoors, seagulls were everywhere there was nowhere for Menna to walk, for fear of harming one of the birds, the whole yard was covered with gulls. Those birds just stood there cawing at me, something the birds were trying to tell me, the birds were fretting , the unrest was evident.

REFLECTIONS OF LIFE

Menna tipped into the house, as Menna looked out of the bedroom window the gulls were perched on the window cawing loudly. Okay, children, said Menna time for dinner, Menna served the children shishkabobs and cobbed corn, of course no cookout is complete without the infamous burger; If allowed, I think the children would have lived off them. About 8:00p.m. the children and me sat down to watch a movie rental, entitled "The Yearling" after the movie the children were bathed and dressed for bed. After the children' prayers and nightly daily message to their dad,(which he would collect on his arrival home), Menna outened the lights. (Each night the children would write out a message to their dad).

That evening while Menna was sitting on the porch relaxing; Menna turned

To look toward the street, the sun had gone down; all of a sudden a family of bats flew right past Mennas' face, if Menna would have turned or moved, she would have rammed her face right into a family of bats, the bats were so close to Mennas' face that she could feel a soft wind on her cheek as the bats flew past. Menna went into the house to do the cookout dishes, Menna had a load of clothes to put into the wash, which had been stained by barbecue sauce; As Menna started down the basement stairs with the laundry; she noticed hundreds of ants making their way up the basement stairs, Menna grabbed a can of insect spray and sprayed, but no matter how many ants she destroyed, that next day there was a more bigger and powerful group of ants. Menna had to call an exterminator.

That night Menna waited up for David, he finally arrived at 12:30; after going over the latest occurrences with him; David replied "what on earth is going on?" Now think honey what are you doing differently than what you were doing, say two weeks ago, asked David. Nothing , said Menna, except I am trying a new soap from the Soaps and More Shop, it is hypoallergenic soap.

Summer was here, during the summer months Menna worked two jobs, she worked for a Psychiatrist and her second job was working at an income tax service. That Monday Menna went in to work at her tax job, by the end of the week the place was infested with huge ants, an exterminator was called in, but the ants would not leave.

Menna left work and drove to the mall, Menna went to the soap shop and discussed the soap with the manager. The Manager and Menna went over a list of ingredients that the soap contained; We found out that the soap contained animal fat; That's' it said Menna to the manager, it must be the soap.. Menna went to her car and on her drive home, there was a bag of something that the children had left in the car, Menna bent over to pick up the bag, and gnats, just started to fill her car. Menna calmly drove home once in the driveway, Menna opened all four windows.

Menna rushed into the house and threw the soap out, The ants continued to multiply, after calling the exterminator three times, the ants did not leave.

Two weeks later, Menna went to check the cellar, and the ants were gone, the gnats were gone. Luther never came back after that, You know God has a way of telling us things, that is every creature in the entire world has a purpose, we have got to stop this, needless killing of animals; As human beings we must cooperate, or we bring about our own destruction.

A POWERFUL HAND LEAPED OUT

NO; a voice said from afar:
As that powerful hand leaped out;
I watched that mighty sword vanish;
Somewhere into the night;
When that powerful hand leaped out;

My life was given back to me,
Without the utterance of a single word;
On that hot summer night;
It was the night I will never forget;
The night that powerful hand leaped out.

FREEDOM FOR THE STALLION

The noise woke me up, children screaming, a woman yelling, oh God, please no more. Menna jumped up running to the phone to call the police; (to Irmas' apartment). Menna checked her own children, they were still fast asleep, it was 4:00a.m., that seemed to be the norm for me, said Menna to herself.

The walls of the highrise are so thin that you can hear silverware drop in the next apartment. Menna knew these late night sounds well. It was Irma and her three children, yelling and screaming. Menna just could not understand Irma, and her silence about everything.

Irma and her husband had moved in about two months ago, when Irma and her family moved in. I kept her three children at my home for two days, while Irma and her husband got settled, and arranged things.

After Irma collected her children, she never called or came by again. That was two months ago, Menna had never even laid eyes on Irmas' husband. It was so strange, he would sneak in and sneak out of the house unnoticed, as if he was trying to hide himself from the world. What was the deep dark secret ?

The children and I awoke the next morning, early, we were going to the zoo, an all day outing, my dad let me use the car. Menna packed lunch, and a change of clothes for the children, and we started on our way by 11:am. The children wanted to have dinner at the zoo, hamburgers, and cotton candy, I agreed, "but just between you and me, I really did not want them to have the cotton candy, since it was their day, I was open to their suggestions.

After a tiring day at the zoo, the children and me pulled into the parking lot of the housing complex. (Mark and Rachel had cotton candy everywhere, all in their hair what a mess).

Menna heard yelling and screaming , confusing words, coming from a window open on our floor. The voice was saying things, like "The end is near, we are all going to die" really weird sounding rhetoric.

Menna looked up and realized that it was coming from Irmas' window, that man must have been her husband, The kids in the playground were making fun of him, and he was threatening them, I had better go and check Irma once the children are looked after; Menna told the area children, "Children behave yourselves, now. We don't poke fun at grownups now do we children, asked Menna?" (No Mrs. Phillips replied the children in unison). We took the elevator up to our floor, got out and headed to our apartment. As Menna ran the childrens' bubble bath, Menna heard bickering coming from the childrens' room. (They were fighting over the top bunk). Bath time children said Menna, the children came running and Menna ushered the children into the bathroom for their bath, bathed them and put on their P>J>s ; Menna gave the children their apple juice, and read them a bedtime story called, "Three Little Pigs", Menna made sure the children went to the rest room, said our prayers and outened the lights. (Looking back Rachel won the top bunk). I guess Mark is a pushover for Rachel, Menna thought".

As Menna called security and explained the situation "Menna asked the officer, could she go ahead of them or should she wait for security to arrive, (security knew me by now, they let me know that they would be over in ten minutes,), I waited.

Security finally arrived, I locked the children in, "I figured they would be alright, I was only going next door, (on second thought, thought Menna, I had better get Mrs. Clark.) Security went ahead of Menna as Menna went to get Mrs. Clark, Mrs. Clark came right over.

When Menna went down to meet security, they knocked on Irmas' door, Irma opened the door immediately as though she was expecting us. Hi Irma said Menna, remember me? "Yes, replied Irma".

Irma, said Menna, I don't mean to pry, but I was just wondering was everything alright? IRMA LOOKED AWAY FROM Menna, with an aggravated look on her voice, Irma muttered under her breath, I knew this was coming.' Excuse me, said Menna. I'm sorry said Irma, please come in, I think that it is time that we talked.

The police and Menna entered Irmas' home, the place was beautiful, thought Menna to herself, so grand. There were Victorian paintings covering the walls and for each painting there was a little miniature pedal stool underneath. The walls were white covered in silver speckles. There was a trophy cabinet full of trophies, Irma and her husbands' furniture was a royal blue, with beautiful ice blue carpet. There were silver, gold and onyx figurines throughout the living and dining area, the wood was beautifully refinished, to a smooth shine.

As Irma motioned for the officer and Menna to sit down, Irma started to explain to us about her husband whose name was Gerald, Gerald is on medication, Gerald is diagnosed as being mentally ill, as long as Gerald takes his medication he is usually calm, but, without the medicine Gerald is irrational and starts saying things that don't make a whole lot of sense. Would you say that Gerald is harmless asked the officer? Gerald hasn't hurt anyone thus far, this is why he is allowed to be home..

I do not know what happened, one day Gerald was a carpenter, and a painter, and the next day he was like this, this is my husband on medication, as Menna looked over at Gerald he was in a daze, not responsive to anything or anybody.

Well Irma, what happened? (asked ,Menna). Well Menna before we moved here, we lived in a warehouse, refurbished by Geralds' own hands.

We were a normal happy family not long ago, my husband had an art class which he taught at one of the colleges. One day said Irma, I was called to pick Gerald up from his teaching job, he had went into a comatose state, he was unresponsive and has been that way ever since.

Gerald has had numerous doctors and psychologists, each one is in agreement that something my husband saw that night had put him into a severe shock state, he was unresponsive and has been that way ever since. All I know said Irma, is that somewhere there lies the key to getting my husband back, all I know said Irma is that I have to keep trying.

REFLECTIONS OF LIFE

Irma, said Menna , I have an idea, I will be in touch with you. Irma do you remember the exact date this incident occurred asked Menna? Sure replied Irma, It was March 20th, I remember, because I had to reschedule the childrens' dentist appointments, But, Irma, said Menna, I heard you yelling and screaming no more was he hurting you? Gerald doesn't get violent said Irma. He starts saying things and uttering phrases that doesn't make any sense, I guess that it can really get to me sometimes.

Well Irma said Menna, I will be in touch with you, how about coffee at my house at 5:00 p.m tomorrow evening, "I'll be there replied Irma.

March 20, Menna heard herself saying as she walked to her car, Menna drove herself to the library, as Menna searched through old newspaper clippings, she found the clippings that was dated March 20th .

Menna thumbed through the headings, Menna found a page which read "more turn up missing". Menna searched for that article, and she began to read.

AS OF MARCH TWENTIETH, THERE WERE TWELVE COLLEGE STUDENTS REPORTED MISSING, BOTH MALE AND FEMALE, NO LEADS HAVE YET BEEN REPORTED.

Now, I remembered that case said Menna, to herself, that case was under investigation seven months ago, and still is, I wonder if Irmas' husband and this case is connected in anyway? Menna jotted down some facts and left. As, Menna drove home, she thought to herself, we could have something here; If only Irmas' husband was alert.

As Menna arrived home, Mrs. Clark was knitting and watching a nite time soap opera, the children were still sleeping. It was 10:00P.M. Menna showered and went directly to bed.

The alarm went off and Menna shot straight up, looked over at her clock, it was 6:a.m., already Menna thought to herself.

The children and Menna readied themselves for school and work, On arrival to school, Menna sent the children to class, and signed herself in. The day seemed to drag by., but we made it through, On the way home, the children and Menna stopped for hamburgers; Menna was expecting Irma at five o'clock, so the hamburgers saved time, besides the children loved hamburgers..

As five o' clock rolled around, Menna prepared coffee and warm danishes for her and Irma. Irma arrived, and Menna asked IRMA in. Irma, said Menna, I went to the library today and checked that date, March 20th of last year, there was o total of twelve college students missing as of that date, from the same college that Gerald taught his art class. Do you think that maybe Gerald would know something, asked Menna? Maybe we can set up something with his psychologist, "I wonder if hypnosis really work (asked Menna).?

Menna, said Irma that could be it, lets' call DR. REDMOND at home and see if we can set up an emergency consult visit, this could be just the break that we need. DR REDMOND WAS ANXIOUS TO GET TO WORK, he was working along with the police department, he set up something for us for that following evening at 7:30p.m., since we both worked and had children.

The weekend finally approached, Irma and Menna dropped the children off at each of their grandparents house, Irmas' parents did not live very far; afterwards we headed for Dr. Redmonds' home office, which he used for weekend emergencies.

Irma took Gerald by the hand and led him in, As Irma and Menna watched through a two-way glass, we saw electrodes being attached to Geralds' head, as he gave him something to help him to relax. Dr. Redmond came out to us, bringing sketches which Gerald had drawn, the sketches were horrific , people in dark robes, people being sacrificed on what looked like an altar of some sort men and women with missing body parts. There was a drawing of a pentagram with the number 212 written underneath it; there was one drawing of people in hoods with shovels.

Irma and Menna left the doctors' office, they hardly talked; Finally Irma said, Menna we have got to take Gerald to this place, "what place, asked Menna". This picture Menna said Irma, this is a picture of an area on the other side of the college, I recognize the barbed wire and that old house, it has been there for years, nobody has lived in that house for at least five years.

Lets' go Irma, as we turned the car around and headed for the college, when, Irma yelled, "hold it Menna, there is a drawing of a clock set for twelve midnight, maybe we should wait till then' said Irma. I think you may have something there, said Menna .

Before going home we stopped at both grandparents home to see if it was alright to leave the children over night, both grandparents (two sets of grandparents) agreed to the arrangements.

After Menna and Irma arrived home, Menna dug out an old pair of hiking boots and some warm clothes, As 11:30 approached, Irma and me decided to put Gerald in bed for the night, We would go out on our own., As we pulled into the old vacant lot, we could see flashes of light, which could be fire, or even flares coming from behind some trees.

We turned the car lights off and headed in the direction of the light, through what seemed to be a tiny forest, /As we drew nearer, we could hear chanting. Stop Irma, Menna said, look ! Right there, not even thirty feet away, were people dressed in black hoods, we saw men, tied to trees, nude tortured bodies of helpless people, being danced around. Irma, said Menna, we had better go for help, We quietly left.

As Menna and Irma pulled into the police station parking lot, we ran to the desk sergeant, telling him what we had witnessed. The policeman did not believe us at first; He assigned two officers to go with us to the site Its' funny when we arrived at the site, no one was there, not even a trace of burning ashes or any other type of evidence that these people had been there. Irma and Menna convinced the officer to come with them that next night at twelve o' clock midnight, we have to be on time said Irma.

That night we were to meet the officers there at that same location. When we arrived the officers, arrived, they ran out through the brush, yelling freeze don't move, there were burnt bodies four of them on stakes, burned beyond recognition. The swat team filled the wagon with all races of people, they were Satanists, we later found out, who sacrificed human beings; the investigating team found charred remains in the cellar of that old house, the number on that house was 212.

We called Dr. Redmond, and explained everything to him, he immediately had Menna and Irma to bring Gerald in for treatment, that following Tuesday. Well, six months later and $100,000.00 worth of treatment fees; Irma moved out of their apartment. Irma and Gerald relocated to a place where Gerald was offered a position as Dean of a well-known college.

That was a frightening experience, totally unbelievable experience that night. I can never forget that smell of human flesh burning.

I guess that Gerald probably had a more frightening experience than we did, Its' funny we never found out why this affected Gerald the way it did, Irma told me that when she went to retrieve Gerald from the college, she noticed rope marks around his wrist and ankles.

Could Gerald have been an intended sacrifice? If so, why was he spared? Even so, why was Gerald allowed to live? I don't have the answers thought Menna to herself

Maybe one day Gerald will feel comfortable enough to talk about it, but for now we just have to go with the way things are now. Gerald and Irma are happy; I often wonder was Gerald affiliated with this cult in any way.

THE BLACK HOLE

As the graduation march came to a sudden halt, "We the graduating class of 1970, took our seats, I heard my sisters and their cheering recruits yelling "yea Menna;, It was somewhat embarrassing. A note found its' way into my lap (Menna), it read "Menna are we going to the graduation party together or as a group; Menna looked down the row at Patrice, as she waved to me, I held my hand up as to say hold on a minute.

After the graduation exercise we threw our caps up in the air, and I looked for our crowd; The graduation was outdoors since the weather was warm. Menna found Patrice, and Collette, we decided to meet there with our dates.

That night before Menna dressed for the graduation party; Mom and dad had their, we are proud of you talk Momma pulled a letter from her apron, I held my breath, this couldn't be the letter I had been waiting for, as I ripped the letter open, my heart started beating faster. I had been accepted, Menna screamed, my first choice, oh momma, Menna hugged her mom and dad.

Menna ran off to her room to finish dressing; Mennas' date arrived ten minutes late; Menna was fifteen minutes, MENNA and DAVID enjoyed soft music and pleasant conversation,

David and Menna had been seeing each other off and on during their senior year, David knew that Menna wasn't thinking along the lines of a serious relationship since we were both planning on going away to college next Fall.

DAVID was a sophomore in college already, we were just good friends for now. David and Menna arrived at the party which was in full force by now, really going strong. MENNA SAW PATRICE AND MICHAEL, AND COLLETTE AND BRAD, Collette and Brad stepped out on the terrace, Menna noticed that Collette was upset about something.

Two couples remaining we danced two dances non-stop; oh dear, I need some air David said Menna, lets go David replied.

Menna and David stepped out on the terrace, there was Collette crying uncontrollably and Brad wasn't around. Menna went over to Collette and asked her why the tears? Collete exclaimed that she was pregnant and Brad claims that it isn't his, and he will be leaving for college in the Fall.

Collette, said Menna, let David leave for college, you are perfectly capable of raising your child, you know that Brad is just that type of human being, give him some time, he will come around. Brad never did come around.

Three years later; Three years have passed since Menna has seen Patrice and Collette, I thought to myself on the bus ride home. I wonder how the girls are doing, said Menna to herself. On arrival home, mom and dad welcomed me, Dad and mom had retired from their jobs by then, It seemed strange having them both at home at the same time,

REFLECTIONS OF LIFE

I called Patrice to let her know that I was home and we could meet at the shake shop at 8:00p.m. I called Collette with the same intent, I could hardly hear Collette over the yelling of their three children, "Menna yelled, Collette, see you at the shake shop. At 8:00p.m., goodbye".

As Menna drove herself to the shake shop, Menna saw Patrice was already there, as our eyes locked we bolted for each other, yelling, and screaming and ju,mping up and down, Patrice let me look at you, said Menna; you haven't changed a bit said Menna, where is Collette?

Girl, the lowdown on Collette, that boyfriend of hers dumped her with three kids and married some other girl from the college. Collette won't be able to make it tonight,. Babysitting problems said Patrice.

"What about you Patrice, said Menna how has life been treating you"? I've been doing good, I am still attending the local college, I landed a job at an advertising agency; Still at home with my parents until I can stabilize my income. I don't have any children yet, maybe one day after my life is more in gear; Patrice replied.

Girl I know what you mean, as far as living home replied Menna, hey why don't we get some burgers' and shakes and take them over to Collettes house, lets treat her and the kids.

We shouldn't bother Collette right now, Collette is having some problems, she needs help, not burgers Collette started to change once Brad left. We are close friends, said Menna, her problems have and will always become our problems, she needs us now, (Collette), Well lets at least call first said Patrice; Done replied Menna,

As we arrived at Collettes' clutching dinner, we were surprised at how long it took Collette to open the door. As Collette opened the door, we held dinner up in the air, surprise we yelled in unison. Come in replied Collette, Collette didn't even look like herself. Collette was unkept, the apartment was full of debris. Collette said Menna, what is going on, this isn't t he Collette I remember, clean yourself up, said Patrice. Collette just stood there unresponsive, Well, said Patrice it looks like our work is cut out for us.

That night we scrubbed and buffed and cleaned for two hours. We gave Collette a new hairdo, and bathed the children and put them to bed, we did not sit down to talk until about twelve midnight. Patrice, said Collette you have got to come out of this depression, you can be happy that at least you have your children, children can offer a lot of happiness, if you would take the time and get to know them.

Menna added; Patrice have you been following up with that therapist that I referred to you? He is really good. Collette replied,

I am fine Menna and Patrice I am just in a slump right now, Brad pays child support, he visits the children; I guess I am just not cut out for motherhood

At that moment Little Brad age three came out into the living room rubbing his eyes; he had wet the bed; Collette became hysterical, yelling and screaming at him; Collette ran over to Little Brad and raised her hand up to hit him , Collette, Menna yelled as Menna ran over to little Brad pushing Collette away. What on earth is wrong with you, yelled Menna? Collette broke down into tears. Collette, I will take the children home with me for a few days I am going to call Brad to come and collect the children, in the meantime , girl, you had better get your act together, these children are not at fault.

Patrice and Menna gathered three sleeping children, and left, we decided that if we couldn't get the Brad to take the children we would have to notify the authorities, we just knew that Collette was in no mental state to handle the children.

We finally got hold of Brad, we explained the situation to Brad and asked him when he could collect the children. Brad replied , give me a few days to work something out with my boss, Will, do Menna replied, Collette had really beautiful children, one boy and two girls, each two years apart, as I watched the children sleep, it was then that I noticed Little Brad's back was covered with bruises. Menna immediately called Brad, and told him that it was an emergency, and that she had to see him. As Brad arrived, he came in, rushed for little Brad, staring at his back in disbelief.

Brad gathered his children up and took them with him that night, his movements were almost mechanical, The next evening, Menna visited with Collette, letting her know that she was there for her, and Menna briefed Patrice on what Collette needed to do. I called the doctors' and set up something for Collette before I went back to school,. So I could make sure that Collette would be there, Patrice was able to take Collette to these appointments, since Patrice lived in town. Menna called Brad and let him know what Collette intended to do,.

Its' funny Menna thought to herself Collette acts' as though she doesn't care about anything, she just sits there with this look on her face, she barely talks, who knows what she's thinking, perhaps the doctor can help her.

As Menna walked to her dormitory, she realized that she was tired. Menna showered and went to bed, Menna felt that she should go up the weekend to check on Collette.

The week dragged by and finally Friday arrived, Menna left Friday at 5:30 and arrived home three hours later. Menna called Patrice, "what's cooking Patrice", Asked Menna, Girl said Patrice,

Brad took the children back to Collette;

What on earth did he do that for, said Menna? Well Menna, said Patrice, you know that Brad has always had a soft spot for Collette, he thinks since she kept a doctors' appointment that she is cured. Alright Patrice, I will be calling on you and Collette about 4:00 tomorrow, meet me at Collettes' will do said Patrice.

As Menna settled down to finish her report, she noticed that it was 3:00a.m.; I'd better get to bed said Menna, boy, what a day.

At 4:am, Menna was awaken by the loud ringing of the telephone, it was Collette, screaming hysterically, Collette what is the matter, asked Menna? Its' little Brad, cried Collette, he is not breathing, I will be right there , said Menna, Menna slammed the phone down and rushed to Collettes' house . The drive seemed so long as Menna tried to get there, to Collettes' house.

On arrival to Collettes' house, Menna banged hard on the door, Collette hurriedly let Menna in; Menna rushed to little Brad's room there laying on the bed was little Brad, his body was all red, and his skin was falling away from his body. My God Collette, what have you done said Menna? Collette pointed to the bathroom, Menna noticed a tub of very hot water, "Collette, yelled Menna, did you put the baby in there, in that hot water, you fool: Collette just stood there dazed, she acted drugged, Menna phoned for an ambulance, Little Brad was dead, Menna could not find a pulse.

Menna looked at Collette for a minute, Menna hated Collette at that moment, Menna walked towards Collette, "Little Brad is gone Collette", Where is he going ? Collette started to hum. Menna tried CPR, maybe he had a chance, he can't be gone, wake up little Brad, please wake up.

That is what I was doing when the ambulance arrived, the paramedics, just pulled me away and covered his burned little body, the other children were unharmed.

Collette, spent two years in a mental institution, I still see Collette, she doesn't even know I am alive, I often time park and watch her sleeping under cardboard boxes. Collette is homeless now, she walks around looking through garbage cans, carrying a shopping bag.

I have not given up on Collette, I'm not finished, I have to figure out a way to bring Collette back to us.

A SECOND CHANCE

Menna first notified the police as to the address, as to where Melanie was supposed to be, On that nightmare drive, I looked for that address. I ran across an old run down building, this can't be it Menna said.

As Menna parked and walked to the building, it was abandoned, this is all wrong. Menna went to the car phone and called her scout, As Menna repeated the address her scout confirmed it, "but there is no one here, replied Menna." Mrs Phillips, Melanie is in there, did you notify the police replied TUT, don't go in there alone, it is a crack house.

She could be, Tut cut Menna off. Mrs. Phillips, I know for a fact that Melanie is diabetic, she gives herself insulin injections. Melanie's parents informed me that Melanie left home without syringes, she has been gone for almost a week now, oh dear, said Menna.

As the police car pulled up, an office came over to Menna, I explained to him about the diabetes, and Melanie being missing for almost a week.

As the officers called for back up, they rushed in knocking, down the door, Menna waited before going in on the advice of the officers, ambulances were on standby.

The place had drug paraphanalia all over the place. This place was not suitable for occupancy of animals or human beings, there was garbage and debris all over the place, stray cats everywhere, the odor was unbearable.

Menna waited as the officers ushered her over to an old wooden crate, Melanie was laying in that crate, packed in ice, Who packed her in ice; yelled Menna, dear God is she alive; as the paramedics rushed over, I heard one say to the other one, "It looks like a diabetic coma", as the paramedics worked feverishly to revive Melanie, I stared in disbelief the paramedics prepared Melanie for transport to the hospital. Menna followed along in her car,Everything was chaotic as I reached the hospital, Menna sat in silence, not believing what she had just witnessed. Menna looked up towards the heavens, she prayed, God I don't know what happened, I don 't know the problem, but You do, God, Melanie has to live, her mom died a horrible death, Melanie has to show us all something, she has to do it for her mom, Please God you have got to save her.   AMEN

As the doctor came out Menna asked him "Will Melanie live"? The doctor informed me that Melanies' body went into shock from lack of insulin, we have to see how she responds to the shots, God must have been with her, her body was not affected at all by the ice. On the contrary the ice kept her alive a little longer, it could have easily went either way.

Melanie is still in a coma, all we can do is wait and hope. Menna called Melanies' grandparents, they rushed right over.

REFLECTIONS OF LIFE

Menna left the Rodgers' there talking to the doctor, as she said her goodbyes, Menna had to go and check her own children.

Mrs. Clark was napping when Menna finally arrived home, the children were fast asleep, as Menna kissed them goodnight, Menna put a blanket over Mrs. Clark and went to bed.

Mrs. Clark was a widow, She often time slept over; always when we would awaken in the morning, she would always be gone. That night Menna thought about Melanie, Menna had to try and prepare a road for her, Menna thought of getting her a job at City Hall, a lot of children worked part-time at these jobs which earned them scholarships to the better colleges. That's' it Menna said to herself. Melanie should do well' she is one of the few kids that the drugs have not affected or destroyed.

That day at work, Menna talked to Dr.Woods, about Melanie; Dr. Woods felt that it was a great idea , she got on the phone right away to the superintendent of schools, and just like that, it was arranged..

Menna visited Melanie everyday for a week before Melanie came to.

That Friday Menna went to see Melanie, to Mennas' surprise Melanie was sitting up and reading a novel. Menna said "Hello, Melanie", good to have you back, "good to be back, replied Melanie. Melanie, said Menna, "I know your grandparents and I grew up with your mom, we were really good friends, your mom and me. Melanie, you look a lot like your mom., what are your plans dear asked Menna as she looked Melanie straight in the eyes. "I intend to finish school and go to college, said Melanie, and to make my grandparents proud of me, I am sorry that they had to go through this, I know that I have acted irresponsibly. "You certainly have, young lady, replied Menna. Melanie I have arranged for you to attend some extensive diabetic classes, and chairperson for the drug awareness program has a job waiting for you. (Melanies' eyes lit up). "I know there are a lot of people who probably didn't have much faith in me about now, said Melanie.

Melanie that isn't important, what is important is that you realize the error of your ways. You know Melanie, when you cut down a tree, it just doesn't stop growing, it continues to root and grow. That is the way that God intended for it to be, you are such a tree Melanie. It doesn't matter if you choose to give up or go on, you will continue to grow as long as God allows, how you choose to use your gift of life, that is something that is left up to you, and if you choose the wrong road, it won't stop you from growing just like that tree.

Thank you said Melanie; Melanie here is my card call me if you need to, any time of the day or night, I will be there; well here are some procedures that you should study and learn, also you will be receiving a letter from City Hall as to the day and time of the orientation, The program is two days a week, and you will receive a paycheck and extra credit for school, Now how does that sound asked Menna.

It sounds like a dream come true said Melanie; so long said Menna as she hugged Melanie, don't forget I am here, said Menna. It sounds like a dream come true said Melanie; So long said Menna as she hugged Melanie, don't forget I am here, said Menna. As Menna left the hospital she kept seeing the light of Melanies' eyes. Menna looked up to the heavens and said "Thank you God, please let it work out, (A voice said she will do it for her mommy).

T^en years have passed since that horrific incident, Melanie followed through and did well.

Well, it is time to get ready for work; Today we are having a guest speaker come to our school, her name is Councilwoman Melanie Rogers, Brown. So you see, Melody's life was not in vain, she left us a legacy, a legacy of love, in spite of every thing. The flowers at Melodys' gravesight, they still bloom year after year.

THE KEY TO CONQUER PAIN AND SORROW

Tell me why does it hurt you, to see things the way they are:
The joy the pain the sorrow
So near and never far;
Sorrow can consume you:
It can rip your heart right out:
The trick is the phrase to conquer;
Which I know we all can endow;
But tell me why does it hurt , To see things the way they are?

Tell Me why does It hurt you to see
Things the way they are:
Love holds the key to the most trivial
Of our fears;
The phrase to conquer; only means to Love;
I should know; since I heard it ;
From way way up above.

Life is what we make it;
We can grow or we can wilt;
But don't tear something down, that the Lord Himself has built.
Pay attention to yourself, and follow,

A very wise man once said;
And then it wouldn't hurt so bad;
No man would ever have to be sad.

A VISITOR

On the way home from work and school, the children and I decided to get dinner from a well-known family restaurant and have dinner in the park, and do our homework, it was a hot day. We played on the swings, and slided, we played hide and seek; and we finally settled down to do our homework before we had dinner.

The children and me were plum tuckered out by 8:00p.m. As we, loaded up to go home, Mark and Rachel and myself joined in singing our favorite song 'The Name Game". Once all loaded up in the car we made our way home;; would you believe that Mark and Rachel did not bicker once.

Mommy, whined Rachel)I spoke to soon, said Menna); What is it Rachel; Mark is pulling my hair, why don't you sit up front with me Rachel. "No that's alright Rachel replied". (Those two stick together like glue Menna said to herself).

Finally, on arrival home, Menna put her key into the door.. , And, as Menna was bending over, something happened, it was like a flash of a picture. Menna started to see Collette, amongst garbage, through a picture in her mind. Menna shook her head, trying to regain her sight, for at least thirty seconds Menna could not see, Menna felt a little dizzy, things were blurry, (What's going on said Menna, I can't see).

Just as abruptly as it came, it went, Menna opened the door to her dwelling place and her and the children entered. Bathtime, Menna said to the children, the children loved bathtime, since a bath just isn't a bath without Mr. Bubble, Mark wash your hair; Rachel don't throw water; c'mon kids to me for a bedtime story.

As the children dried off Menna quickly moisturized them, Helped them get into their sleepers, gave the children warm milk to help them wind down, tucked the children in real tight and we prayed. Amen, yelled Rachel; Mark trying to be a little more reserved, just yawned.

Everybody asleep said Menna as she finished up their bedtime story, "The little engine that could" Finally the children were fast asleep. Menna,,glanced at her watch, it was 9:30.

 good said Menna as she showered and relaxed on the sofa with a cup of herbal tea. As Menna sat there she kept hearing Collettes' name in the back of her mind, over and over again, Mennas' thoughts went back to Collete and how close they were.

When Menna first moved to this town , Collette was the first friend she had who showed her around. Buffalo was so much different from California;. Collette was the one to tell Menna, don't say soda, here we say pop, otherwise people will think you are weird,. Collette was practically the only one who did not laugh at the way I walked or talked,. I guess you could call Collette my teacher.

I guess we drifted apart when Collette started hanging around with a different group of people. I really worried about Collette. She was so naïve. I guess you could say that Collette believed in fairy tales; That handsome prince that Collette was trying so desperately to find to come and carry her off and they would live happily ever after. I guess that is when Brad came along, Collette and Brad were like magnets, they were so attracted to one another. I guess you could call Brad , Collettes' knight in shining armor; luckily for Collette that Brad was a little more realistic about life; Brad was in high school; he was different; one day he just said, that I am tired of hanging out, time to grow up now and that is just what Brad did.

In spite of the abuse that Collette had suffered, at the hands of her stepfather, Menna always thought that Collette would rise up above it. Abuse is a very bad thing, it has been going on for many years, that was the real reason that God destroyed Sodom and Gomorrah back in biblical days. In fact that was the reason why God brought about all destruction.

I guess that is about the time when Menna began to realize that she could see and feel things, like the pain and sorrow of others.

I went to visit Collette one day, I felt the presence of something unclean, Menna could not even eat the food. She felt nauseous on entering her home. (Collettes' home). Collettes' mother and stepfather were in the family room, Collette and Menna went to Collettes' room to hear her records; as Menna walked into Collettes room, pictures started flashing in front of Mennas' eyes, pictures of Collette and her stepfather having sex on Collettes' bed. Collette was standing right behind me and she never even saw it.

Menna felt better after she was outside; Collettes stepfather was concerned, he ran after me to the first floor; Menna looked into his eyes, she didn't say anything, it was a feeling that let him know that from here on in he would be exposed, and he was, without even a word..

Menna could feel the presence of satan and I see him laughing at all the poor lost souls.

Menna left Collettes' house and went directly to the fathers' against violence; If Collette was afraid to report, I wasn't going to be. Menna talked to one of the elders, a wise man who listened without saying a word. His face was always so expressionless, you never knew what he was thinking, it was as if he didn't hear you or a word you were saying.

The fathers' never intruded on a persons privacy, they secretly operated, nobody really understands how these situations are handled, but Menna and others knew that the kids were safe. The children did not get away with anything, but we were safe. Menna never knew what happened, all she knew was that the stepfather admitted his error and was forced outside of the home.

He eventually left town, The fathers arranged for extensive counseling for Collette and her mother, One elder became a big brother figure to Collette and an advisor to Collette and her mom, they made them feel special again and up to this day.Collette still refers to them as her dad. They taught Collette the meaning of what it meant to have a father.

I guess that's how she met Brad, Brad was the elders' son. Brad was really good for Collette, Brads' marriage was annulled while in school. I guess he realized that it was a mistake and that he still loved Collette. Thinking back, Menna could not help but ask herself why did Collette give up so easily. Collette had so much going for her.

Menna stared at her watch; my goodness said Menna it is already 7:00am; children time for school; C'mon lets' get a move on Menna hurriedly dressed the children, we ate eggs and waffles for breakfast, and was on our way. Children , Menna said on the way to school, it is Friday, any suggestions for the weekend? We want to go to Darien Lake yelled Mark and Rachel. Okay, kids said Menna, lets' go Saturday and have a picnic. How does that sound.

YEAH: yelled the children. As Menna and the children entered the school building, Menna noticed that she and the children were on time.. Good morning Menna said as she greeted the class. "Good Morning said the children in unison". The day just dragged on, but finally it was time to go home. That Friday evening the children and I cooked hot dogs and hamburgers on the grill, we spent most of the afternoon in the park. It was just too hot to go indoors.

The park was directly across the street from our home. As a matter of fact, you could see our windows from our favorite picnic area. We did our homework after our picnic and we went indoors.

There was a breeze stirring; living in a highrise, we could leave windows open while being away from home. It felt comfortable in the apartment, with the front and back windows open, it cooled off considerably.

The children and Menna bathed, and showered, and watched a movie on television, and enjoyed popcorn and ginger ale during the duration of the movie, The movie entitled "Mac and Me" lasted about two hours, the children were asleep before the movie was even over.

Menna put the children to bed, and went over the days mail. It was 10:15, so Menna laid the childrens' clothes out for school, and went over the weeks school-work. Menna waxed the floors, since the children were asleep, and finally Menna climbed into bed herself. Almost instantly Menna had drifted off to sleep.

That Saturday morning was full of excitement, we had a light breakfast of fruit and cereal; I gave the children a pastry, by then it was time to pack the car. It was 9:30a.m.

The children and me dressed and went out to pack the car and take the bus to the Lake, to enjoy the scenic route, we arrived at the Lake at about 11:30. Menna had packed drinks and plenty of fruit, the children will eat dinner at the Lake; Today was the day to pay one price at the family rate and ride free all day, that left us dinner, money.

The ride on the bus to the lake was relaxing, it felt good to relax and let someone else do the driving for a change; The children were full of excitement, The children rode ponies, steered little cars, played in the wading pool, boy did they have fun; Menna took pictures of the Ninja Turtles in person with the children. What a thrill that was for the kids; The children rode ponies steered little cars, played in the wading pool, boy did they have fun; Menna took pictures of the Ninja Turtles in person with the children, What a thrill that was for them the children rode the merry-go round, and visited sea world, those kids went on non-stop till 4:00p,m, with their occasional snack bar stops.

At 6:00p.m the children and Menna found a grassy spot. The children laid down and napped for about forty-five minutes, By seven'o clock we had dinner, by 7:45 p.m. we were heading for home; the children were plum tuckered out. Finally Menna and the children arrived at the bus terminal and headed for the car.

Menna had already loaded the sleeping children into the car, as Menna started to load the bags into the car. She looked behind her, and there was Collette; Collette had shopping bags full of old rags and newspapers, she had a skull cap on in extremely hot weather, her hands were covered with gloves with the fingers cut out, she was wearing an old wool coat.

Tomorrow was Sunday, Menna made up her mind that she would find Collette This Sunday, the children would be spending with their grandparents. That afternoon Menna took Mark and

REFLECTIONS OF LIFE

Rachel to their grandparents house, Mark and dad were working on a kite Rachael was learning to make cookies, so the children were looking forward to going.

As Menna walked through the bus station, she asked around for Collette , nobody could tell Menna anything. Menna went to the areas where the homeless lived, she tried the missions; she searched high and low, but no Collette, it would be dark soon, I will never find her then, said Menna to herself..

It was nearly 8:00p,m, ,Menna stopped into a coffee shop and ordered coffee, she finished her coffee, stopped at the checkout register to pay, as Menna rummaged through her jacket lining for money, she happened to look up and noticed Collette, on the outside of the big plate glass window , looking in..

Menna hurriedly put two dollars on the counter top and rushed out after Collette; "Where did she go asked Menna, as she looked up and down the street, Menna saw her, she quickly ran up to Collette, "Collette yelled Menna, Collette just stared, she never said a word. Menna put her hand out hoping that Collette would come with her, Menna was going to take Collette to get a hot meal with her. As Menna and Collette sat down to eat, Menna asked Collette to come with her, Collette needed medical attention, Collette had opened. Infected sores all over her legs, the odor was atrocious.

After Menna paid for the dinner Collette and her headed for Menna's car, Menna did not realize how far away the car was. It was over an eight block radius.

As Menna and Collette walked to the car, Menna noticed a feeling of uneasiness walking in that part of town. We are almost there, Menna said to Collette, as they approached the car, two dark figures jumped out from the shadows, they seemed to know Collette, they snatched Collettes bags and started looking for something, Collette turned to run, Menna jumped in front of Collette., at that moment, Menna began to feel pressure in her abdomen, Menna looked down and saw her blood and the handle of the knife, protruding from her stomach, Menna had been stabbed. ,Menna fell to the ground, hearing a faint female voice. saying " is she alive"? There was another male voice saying "lets get out of here.

Menna awoke to the antiseptic smell of the hospital. The doctor told Menna that she was lucky, if the knife had of been disturbed you could 've had some serious permanent injuries, it could have costed you your life. The healing process would last at least a week. Menna phoned her parents and reassured them that she would be alright, Mennas' mom and dad, and the children rushed right over, along with the Fathers' against violence members.

Mom just looked at Menna and shook her head as if to say' why does she take such chances' Mom took the children out and then came the lecture via my father , (Now, you did it Menna said to herself.

As Menna awoke that morning, she was looking right into her husbands face, he looked so handsome in is military gear. Hi, honey said Menna, I guess you heard what happened, I just thank God that you are alive, "replied David". Menna, never take another chance like that ever again, said David., I promise said Menna

David and Menna kissed and talked about the children, and kissed some more, all of a sudden Menna felt protected again, she felt she could relax a while.

Menna told David about Collette, David was shocked,. David said that he had been in touch with Brad and Brad was worried sick over Collette. He wants Collette home with him and the children.

`David told Menna to relax and things would be alright, he and the Fathers Alliance was going after Collette. The men were very angry that they were not informed sooner and Menna felt two feet tall.

The Earth Has Eyes

Can you recognize life as the way it should be?
Then open your eyes and see;
The children who have not yet been found;
This is serious, because God wears a frown,

The sufferage and pain is to much to bear;
When a child cries out and no one is there;
Pain, fear, Death still to be carried out:
Until that gift of love, no longer is locked out.

THE SILENT CRIES

I don't like this one bit, why close the incinerator down anyway; Now I have to go all the way down to the dumpst er; Once a month the incinerator closed down for two days to clean out the ashes, what an inconvenience., said Menna. C'mon kids let's go for a walk to the dumpster downstairs;

I guess that day just turned out wrong, Collette had disappeared again; Collette had gone home, but Collette continues to leave home for days at a time without a word; Brad was worried all the time about Collette.

Collette is one of the few people who has everything to live for. The doctor who Collette sees, says that Collette has a slight contusion on her brain, which has healed, but the dead tissue must be removed and Collette would be as good as new.. Sometime ago Collette must have hit her head and never seeked medical treatment. That explains a lot of irrational behavior, behavior that dates all the way back to the tragic death of her son. Medical attention is very important.

The surgery is costly but there is hope for Collette. Brad still wants to marry her, in spite of it all. Cmon kids lets' take the stairs up! Its' good exercise; As the children and I raced up the stairs; I heard muffled cries; As the children and I neared our dwelling place the cries became louder and clearer; These are baby's cries , Menna said as her and the children neared the door.

I saw it; a brand new baby in a big basket, with a note; Oh my goodness; Menna said; what have we here, Look Mark and Rachel; (My dolly said Rachel); No Rachel this is a baby; a life. I looked at the tiny little baby, with his big eyes, and smooth beautiful skin; as pure as the driven snow; I thought; untarnished and perfect in every way.

I carefully unfolded the note; the note read "Please care for this little boy, This is one that they won't get". There was a metal trinket of some sort pinned to the baby, it was cut down the middle, it could have been a half of a heart shape or something of that nature.

The children and Menna went inside the house with the bundle; Menna carefully sat the baby in his basket on the desktop, and phoned the police.

Menna wondered to herself, what could this possibly be about. Just then the phone rang Menna answered the telephone with a quick hello. Menna heard voices in the background, but no one said anything; Suddenly the phone went dead, abruptly.

The authorities finally arrived for the bundle, and I showed them the note and the half of trinket; I also told them about the strange phone call I had just received.

As the authorities left with the baby and the evidence that I had, I searched my mind and I asked myself, could Collette in anyway be involved in this; It just seemed to come at that time when Collette was on my mind.

I felt that I needed to return to the place where I had found Collette before, and find out if she knew anything about his ; however; I thought about Collettes' condition; She just snaps in and out of reality at a moments notice; Its' funny when Collette is in her right mind she talks with sensibility; but when she goes off into her world no one can get through to her.

I wonder does Collette remember signing her consent for the surgery she needed. I know that I had to focus on Collette, because time was running out; Collette should have been in the hospital as of now, for pre-testing. I heard the glass break. I looked around and Rachel was on top of the cabinet trying to get the cookies; (That brought me back to my senses). Cut out the day-dreaming Menna said to herself; Mark and Rachel come and help me make dinner. "Maybe, that will keep them out of trouble", (Menna thought to her-self).

While the children and I sat down to a meatloaf dinner we chatted about our new arrival; Mommy can I keep the baby doll? (Asked Rachel) I don't want a new baby said Mark; Now children that is not our baby, he belongs to someone else, we have to find out who that baby belongs to and give him back,

That night Menna and the children all pitched in to do the dinner dishes. Menna noticed how excited the children were about the little baby, "Kids calm down, said Menna, the baby is safe now; we probably won't ever see the baby again, ": You see ,,the baby has to go back home to his real mommy and daddy; "Mommy who is going to find the mommy and daddy; said Mark. The kids' police will, of course, replied Menna.

Menna finally got the children settled down with a bath and a story. And finally it was off to bed for the children.

Today was Friday, so no homework. As Menna was puttering around picking up toys, and putting away games: the phone rang; I looked at the clock, it was 9:15p,m, "Hello said Menna, as she answered the phone". (Menna said a voice on the other end of the phone.) "Yes , replied Menna". My name isn't important, said the voice). How did you get my number asked Menna"? (The strange voice replied, I can look in a phone book"). Why are you calling me asked Menna?" (Collette used to talk about you an awful lot, I felt that I needed to contact you to let you know about Collette; You see Collette is getting deeper and deeper into something extremely dangerous, which could cost her , her life. Please give me specifics,said Menna (It is Collette; Collette is sometimes aware of what is going on around her; but most of the time she is in another world. It was during that time that a male and female started using Collette to pick up and deliver newborn babies; Most of the women are either homeless or addicts and cannot take care of the babies anyway, so they sale their children for quick cash; These people in turn sale the babies to others, anyone who wants a baby; without even looking into the situation; they don't care about these innocent children. About a month ago books turned up missing with the names and addresses of woman on their payroll, who made a living out of having and selling these babies. They suspect Collette, because Collette had started seeing things that she could not go along with.

Babies have been taken directly from the mothers, and placed into the hands of the police. Is Collette around you? Do you know where I can find her?(replied Menna); None of us night people have seen Collette in about three days; That is unusual, this is why I am calling you. Oh dear , Menna said to herself", I thank you for calling me, if you hear from Collette, please contact me at this number, do you have the number? (Menna asked). Yes replied the strange voice; "Is there any way I can reach you replied Menna?" (I will be in touch replied the voice); Suddenly the phone went dead.

Menna called the police directly, and let them know what she had found out; Menna also reported Collette missing. Now what shall I do: I guess I should let Brad know what is going on. I picked up the phone to call Brad. Hello Brad, said Menna< Menna began immediately filling Brad in on the details, as to what was going on with Collette. Brad did not respond the way Menna had expected him to, how strange. Brad , what if Collette is dead?

I do not want to think that way said Brad, I have to contact the fathers' alliance; I think that we need to do some foot work , Menna, I will keep you informed said Brad. As Menna hung up the phone, she could not help but to think about Brad's reaction; He just struck me as being to calm about this, I don't know, things just don't even out to me.

I was instructed not to interfere by officials, all Menna could do was pray and wait; (Dear God, said Menna, things just keep coming up an d not pleasant things, is Collette alright? How can I help? What can I do? I don't know God, it just seems like I should be doing something . You told me to obey the laws; so now all I can do is sit here and ask you to protect Collette, that's all I can do.   AMEN

Just at that moment at 11:15p.m. the phone rang; Menna ran to answer the phone; Hello said Menna, the voice on the other end of the phone said (Menna, I am alright, and quickly hung up).

Collette, Menna yelled (to late, the phone went dead)   As Menna held on to the phone, yelling Collettes name., I could not believe it: Was that Collette or someone else, who sounded like her. Menna laid on the sofa and drifted off to sleep.

That morning Menna woke up to the static of the television, which she never turned off the night before. Menna looked at the clock, it was 7:00 a.m., Menna jumped up running to wake the children, then she finally realized that it was Saturday, Menna layed back down until the children woke up.

This was their Saturday to spend the day with their grandparents, they were going to the museum, and out to dinner; so today was supposed to be my day of rest; But how can I rest. (I pray that it was Collette who called, last night, at least Menna knew that she was alright). The children finally woke up, we had breakfast at 10:am and dressed; the children finally woke   The children were full of energy and excitement, at 1:00p.m. we were going to a parade. The children were going to their grandparents after the parade.

Stop it Mark yelled Rachel, Mommy, mommy, Mark is pulling my hair, (No I'm not , said Mark;) Kids come on, said Menna, it is time to go to the parade. Mark and Rachel were so taken by the clowns, and the acrobats that were in the parade; we took tons of pictures; Mark and Rachel looked on in awe; everything was so beautiful, the bright colors and the beautiful costumes; "The circus was on parade". And what a beautiful sight it was.

Finally the clowns performed a juggling act before the crowd, there was a little dog jumping in and out of hoops; Then the man on stilts handed suckers out to the children; Mark and Rachel sat there staring in amazement. They were glued to their spots.. I don't ever remember seeing these two children so quiet for so long, I never thought it was possible.

Three o' clock p.m. nearing the end of the circus parade. Menna told the children that we had better get going , since there grandparents were expecting them at there by 3:30p.m.

All at once Rachel, started yelling, I don't wanna go; grabbing on to the pole of a no parking sign., holding on for dear life.

Rachel, please let go, said Menna, don't you want to go and see the dinosaur bones, "no, yelled Rachel, I want to stay here". Alright then Rachel, said Menna, we will just stay here then, all night,

Rachel, said Mark, you always have to go and spoil things; mommy, let's just leave Rachel here, whined Mark. Don't be ridiculous Mark, said Menna, "Okay , Rachel, said Mark, we can share Pugsley, I will let you feed him, (Pugsley was Marks' pet turtle, Mark never let Rachel go near his turtle, now Mark was willing to share his pet turtle with Rachel, if that don't beat all.) "I can hold him to , said Rachel?" Yep, said Mark, for a long time, okay lets' go, said Rachel. As Menna pulled out of the parking lot, she breathed a sigh of relief, (I thought, we would have been there all day, that Rachel can surely be stubborn.).

My parents were at the door I sent the children in, I would visit another time, that incident at the parade, meant t he children would be late for their outing.

Hi mom, hi'dad, said Menna, will call you later. (Okay dear said mom. We will bring the children home tomorrow afternoon . Mark, Rachel (said Menna), be kind to your grandparents, I will see you tomorrow. "Bye mommy the kids said".

As Menna pulled out of her parents, driveway, she felt that she could at least go home to be near a phone. As Menna put her key in the door, to her surprise, the door was opened. Menna looked inside, the place was ramsacked, it looked as though someone may have been looking for something. Menna, phoned the police, the police arrived, and took a report . Menna remembered the card the investigator had given her, when she reported the baby,. I wonder if anything had turned up, thought Menna.

Menna dialed the number on the card the investigator had given her, when she reported the baby, I wonder if anything had turned up, thought Menna. Menna dialed the number on the card and asked to speak to Leutenient Calhoun; The leutenient reassured Menna that they were working on the case, and there was nothing that he could disclose to her as of yet

Mennas' spirits suddenly dropped, when Menna phoned Brad and pretty much got the same response. The phone rang just at that moment, (Hello, said Menna). It was that strangers' voice on the other end of the phone. "I have an address that you might be interested in, said the stranger, you are to go there promptly at 7:30p.m., and please be on time. Suddenly the phone line went dead.

By 7:00p.m. Menna was ready to go to this address. 7645 Meadowlane; As Menna pulled up in front of the newly built home, Menna told herself "Menna, what are you doing? You just don't go to strange homes like that, maybe you should blow the horn and wait for someone to come out," Menna did just that.

Menna looked at the door as she blew her loud horn, Menna saw the door open and an elderly couple stepped out onto the porch, and looked around for the blowing horn. Hello Menna shouted from her car; the couple looked Mennas' way as they waved Menna over to them. Menna walked over to the couple; (Are you Menna Phillips?) "

"Yes, who are you replied Menna". We are the grandparents of the child you found, and we would like to personally thank you, please come in, said the elder gentlemen. They led Menna to the babys' room, he was fast asleep in a nice quiet, comfortable. newly remodeled room.

We have been searching for our grandson for weeks, our daughter is not well, we felt that we had to thank you. We are Mr. And Mrs. Raymond Scott, we reported our grandson missing about two weeks ago, we have had custody of our grandson since he came into the world three months ago. My daughter is living out there on the streets by choice, she knows that we are here for her.

What is your daughters' name asked Menna? (My daughters name is Kate, Kate Scott. And before I forget, I have something for you. Mrs. Phillips I was advised to return this to you; (said Mrs. Scott), as she handed Menna the half metal trinket.

Who instructed you to return this to me, asked Menna? I cannot disclose that information to you said Mrs. Scott, But, I have been instructed to tell you to relax and someone will contact you in seventy-two hours.

As I left the Rodgers' home, everything seemed so strange, so unreal to Menna.

Something is missing. I am confused, this just doesn't sit right with me. I needed to know what was going on, the whole story, but no one was willing to talk.

That Saturday afternoon, my parents brought the children home and visited a while; I didn't tell them anything. And I didn't want them to worry. I figured I would tell my parents when I had more details. I suppose, I would have to be patient, thought Menna. My parents and me talked about the children and the things that children get into. Dad was trying to teach Mark how play chess, and Rachel was learning to knit. I sat correcting papers for Monday. I felt safe with both my Parents there. I really enjoyed there weekend visits, so did the children.

Finally it was 9:00p.m. usually that was the time my parents packed up to leave. Mom always bathed and bedded the children before they left. That Sunday the children and I were going to ride up to the base to spend the day with the childrens father. I guess that that would be our few hours of peace, away from everyone, besides, I had some news For David; Menna was three months pregnant by her doctors' calculations, David and Menna had talked about her and the children moving out to the base, so they all could be together, however we decided against it since our jobs and families were in Buffalo. Besides, we spent alternating weekends together, so it was alright and working out for us.

At 11:00p.m. Menna said time for the news; I said aloud; I turned on the news channel and staring at me wasw the Mayor of Buffalo; Letting everyone know to be patient; Things are a bit restricted as of now. The mayor went on tosayt problems will be cleared up shortly, please be patient, That struck a note in me; Somehow Menna ; Somehow Menna guessed that it let her know that everything would be alright. Menna dozed off to sleep I guess for the first in a long while, we felt some sense of peace. Menna noticed a soft gold light that had overcome the room it carried a sense of serenity with it. That Sunday the children and I were up early by 9:am; as we dressed carefully and got ready for our three hour bus ride, I could see how excited the children were about spending the day with their father; I packed fresh baked goods; " a peach cobbler from my mother in law, apple turnovers from my parents, and a coconut cake, compliments of Menna, Mark, and Rachael. The kids and I often parked the car and took the bus to the base.

On arrival to the base David was there waiting, The children ran over to him, David grabbed the children up in a big bear hug; I was a little more composed. I just walked real fast; "Hi honey, said Menna as she pecked David on the lips; Hey, Muffins' said David; (What's in the basket?) Just some baked goods from our parents, and a Coconut cake compliments of the children and myself. replied Menna. Well honey what's' on the agenda , asked Menna; "well honey, lets' start off with a bus tour, and then a little bowling, and dinner. I have reserved one of the Towne Houses for you and the children., said Davids he picked up the bags. Okay troops lets' hit it, said David, as we marched to the jeep.

Finally on arriving at the Towne House, Menna placed the baked goods in the refrigerator, and took a shower, while David and the children put together a jigsaw puzzle. It was about 2:00p.m. by then. Menna said okay Mark and Rachel lets' take our 45 minute

Nap, so that we can be all refreshed for our tour, and dinner. Ah, mommy I want to play with daddy, whined Mark, me too chimed Rachel.

Now children, said David, lets' not give mommy a hard time; Awww said, Rachel

And Mark, lets' go kids David said as he bedded down the children.

Asleep finally, said Menna as she looked in on the children; Menna sat down on the loveseat next to David and started telling him about the strange things that had been goiu

Going on at home; David groaned; and said , Menna have you been behaving yourself? "Yes, replied Menna, it has been hard, but I have been obeying the laws; Good, said David, now just be patient, and soon things will clear themselves up.

David, said Menna, you act as if you know something that you are not telling me. Sweetheart, replied David, I am only repeating what the mayor said; There you go Menna being a skeptic again. Yes, I suppose you are right David, said Menna, but, David, I have something more important to tell you. What is that , said David. Oh nothing, just that I am three months pregnant by my doctors' calculations.

Oh that's' good dear David said as he continued to read the newspaper; "Ahm what. Said David a few moments later, high excitement in his voice? That is the best news yet, said David, as he picked Menna up off of her feet and gently turned her around several times.

Finally the clock alarm went off, it was time to wake Mark and Rachel exclaimed Menna.

David and Menna woke up the sleepy children. Menna gave the children chocolate milk and hot dogs, washed their faces and changed their clothes, dressed myself and then we were ready to go.

First we rode on the family tour bus around the base. And surrounding areas; the landscaping was beautiful; lovely rich green grass; everything was so neat; not so much as a candy wrapper on the ground.. After the tour, which lasted for one hour, w4e got off at the PX, which, was where the bowling alley was located. Mark and Rachel, teamed up against David and me at first, and then it was Menna and Mark, and Rachel and her dad. We bowled about six more games before it was time for dinner; we led the kids to believe that we tied the score, when in reality, David and Rachel won..

Web rode a shiny new jeep to the family restaurant in town; David and me had the Western Burger with fries. Later we would have dessert in our room, or maybe the family dining room at the hotel.

After we had dessert it was 8:30p.m., time for the children and me to get ready for our bus ride home; So as to board the bus by 10:00p.m. My brother in law always met us at the bus terminal to help me to get the children home safely, since Mark and Rachel were always sleep at that time. Ryan my broth4er in law always followed behind in his car.

Ryan carried the children up, since they were asleep; I gave Ryan some magazines that he had asked David to send him. Ryan had a quick snack and was all set to go back on duty; (Ryan was a detective with Central Intelligence. Finally, it was my turn to relax, as Menna pulled out fresh school clothes for the children, for the following day, she noticed that it was almost three'o clock a.m. (Hopefully I will be in bed by 3:30, Menna thought to herself).

Menna checked the answering machine, there was a number on the answering machine for Menna to call. Menna quickly dialed the number. Hello, said Menna; (Menna immediately recognized the strangers voice).

Yes said Menna I am returning your phone call. The stranger replied: "I have a message For you, you are to go to Saint Josephs'

REFLECTIONS OF LIFE

Hospital, Monday (tomorrow) at 12:30 in the afternoon, you will stop at the front desk and sign your name as Menna Phillips; Make sure you take valid identification along. From there you will be escorted to the designated area. Yes, I will be there said Menna: suddenly the phone rang, and went dead, even my phone was dead that time; Menna put the receiver of her phone into its' cradle, when Mennas' phone rang one time, when Menna picked up the phone there was a dial tone. Weird o rama, I thought to myself; I thought about the children and my visit with David. He acted as if he knew what was going on, when I told him of the new occurrences in my life. Oh well, Menna said as she dismissed the thought from her mind. Wow am I tired, thought Menna; Menna went to bed, she quickly drifted off to sleep.

That morning the children were really impossible to deal with. Mark and Rachel argued for every little thing; just snapping at one another. Alright kids; if you are good in school today, I will take you to your favorite McDonalds after school. Yea, yelled the children. Hey kids you have to be good this morning too, and you have to stop arguing with each other. Okay mommy said Mark and Rachel. Okay now Mark, said Menna, help your sister pack up her books, Rachel you go get Mark and your jackets. Now children anymore bickering, and no Ronald Mc Donald is that understood? "Yes mommy, said Mark and Rachel". The kids were nice as pie the rest of the day.

On our arrival to school, I sent the children to class, and let the principal. "Dr. Woods", know that Mrs.Griffin would be covering for me this afternoon. I had an errand to go on.

On my drive to Saint Josephs' Hospital, I thought to myself, "I have no recollection, as to why I am going here." As Menna pulled in to the parking lot of the hospital, she found a parking space close to the front entrance.

Menna walked into the hospital, and walked up to the front desk. Menna gave the clerk her name, and after waiting for about five minutes, a nurse came down, and asked Menna for identification; Menna pulled out her drivers license and handed it to the clerk, in turn the clerk passed the license over to the nurse. The nurse motioned Menna to follow her . Menna followed the nurse onto the elevator up to the top floor, As Menna walked off the elevator, with the nurse leading her, Menna was escorted to a private room. Menna did not think that this was a room since the label on the door read "storage area." Security was everywhere.

Menna followed the nurse through the door and then through another set of doors. Menna could not believe her eyes, there was Collette in a hospital bed with electrodes affixed to her head. Menna could not tell if Collette was conscious or not.

What is wrong with her asked Menna; Collette is fine replied the nurse. She has had some very delicate brain surgery. She is going to be just fine. The surgery was a success and this young lady will be her old self again.

When will she be coherent? Said Menna to the nurse; Why don't you give her at least two weeks, to complete the healing process. How did Collette get here? asked Menna. Collette was escorted here via the police. Collette is under police protection around the clock. Collette has been here for almost one week.

"Mrs. Phillips, Collette asked me to give you this" said nurse Rawlins as she handed Menna an envelope. Menna looked on in surprise as she ripped open the envelope. Inside the envelope was the other half of the trinket. Menna scrambled through her purse for her part of the trinket. Menna found the trinket and put the pieces together.

TO BE CONTINUED...

COUNT YOUR BLESSINGS

He threw a letter to the floor, as Menna stared at the letter, she recognized the military stationary. Where did you get this from? Yelled Menna, the man spun Menna around and grabbed her around her throat, Mennas' back hit the wall, Menna heard the man say, who besides you is in the house? Menna yelled out no one. As he violently threw Menna towards the back of the house, Menna wondered to herself, where are the children?

The stranger grabbed Menna by both shoulders, slamming her up against the hallway wall. Now listen to me he said, you are going to do just as I say. It was then , that Menna saw his switchblade coming towards her face, he waved the obscene looking thing in front of Mennas' face , it was with that hand that he took his arm and pinned Menna to the wall, then he started unbuttoning his coat, Menna remained silent.

All of a sudden Mennas' five year old came running out of his room with a plastic bat, running towards this stranger, yelling "leave my mommy alone"... Oh God No, Menna yelled with tears streaming down her face. Talk fast a voice said from out of nowhere. As Mark kept coming, I said, I don't know you sir, but please don't hurt my baby, I will do anything. The noise must have startled him because he released his grip on Menna, as Marks bplastic bat came down on the back of his leg. He turned towards my son., Menna pushed past him yelling no! Menna quickly scooped Mark up in her arms and ran for the childrens' room to get my daughter.r, with each step Menna pictured a switchblade being buried in my back, I had to make it thought Menna

Menna ran with her son in her arms to the childrens' room Menna grabbed the door, as Menna slammed the door , with this giant of a man standing there with a switchblade up in the air, Menna quickly locked the door. Oh God what shall I do, said Menna, Mennas' letter opener flashed through her mind.

Menna started throwing boxes off the shelf of the closet, while the intruder kicked in the door, Menna finally located the letter opener, well-hidden from the children. The door started to give in, Menna yelled; "Oh My God", putting the children behind her Menna told Mark to take Rachels' hand and when I tell you to run, you run to Ms. Grace house and ask her to call the police. The door was slowly falling off the hinges, Menna , Menna yelled for the man to come on, the door came crashing down, something was wrong, he didn't come in. Menna heard comotion, and things breaking outside the door of the childrens' room, somewhere, I had to investigate. Children stay here.

Menna went to the door of the bedroom, and peeked out. Menna heard scrambling and crashing, commotion, as She climbed over the shrubbel, Menna made her way to the front of the house,. Menna was yelling to Rachel and Mark, telling them to hide under the bed.

Menna nervously placed her back up against the wall of the hallway leading to the front of the house, letter opener in hand. Menna slid down the length of the hallway ever so quietly. Menna took the last step into the family room,. Menna saw the back of a stranger standing over the intruder, holding him down. The police were here.

The police explained to Menna that they were in the neighborhood investigating the mailbox breakins, when we pulled into the lot downstairs, we heard the commotion and noise coming from this window we had to investigate and make sure that you were alright.

Menna ran to her children and scooped them up in her arms. Mommy are we still going to granmas, asked Rachel? Sweetheart we are all going to stay home and thank God for our blessings.

WHY IT WAS A PERFECT FIT

Menna began to read the letter, it read,

> *Dear Menna,*
> *I am sorry that you had to be put through this. In three weeks Brad and I will be getting married, I would like for*

you to be my maid of honor. Brad and I will be getting married in the chapel here at this hospital. It seems that everyone believes that would be safer and better for my health. I do not know when I will be able to live my life normally again. That is up to the authorities. I don't even know how long I will be under guard here at the hospital. The wedding is March 14th at 2:00 p.m. We will talk then.

Love,
Collette

Menna looked heavenward and said, "(Thank you my heavenly father, this is the most wonderful gift imaginable. In three weeks Collette and Brad were going to be married. Thank you God for hearing me, and most of all thank you for not being ling in answering.)   Amen

Menna was so overwhelmed with joy that she sang all the way home. On arrival home Menna put her key in the door to let herself in. Menna still had an hour before it was time to pick up the children, just enough time to freshen up, thought Menna.

As Menna walked inside her home, she looked up and saw David standing there, along with two uniformed officers. "What is going on honey?" said Menna to David. "Relax, Muffins" said David to Menna. Everything is just fine now. You see Menna a few months ago I suspected that you might be pregnant, I could not risk you or the children being harmed.

We went after Collette and found out that a baby-selling ring was operating in our fair city; after tracking that couple, the same people that assaulted you, this man and woman team led us to some powerful worldwide contacts. This black-market practice had been secretly operating here. Using our town as home base. They made one mistake they fell for our plan. Collette has been working undercover with the police force for about six months now. This is how we single-handedly crushed their operation. Over two hundred arrests were made statewide.

We were confused at first; we could not understand why we could not track them right away. We kept losing them. We could not figure out how new arrivals were in and out of the city before we could tie our shoe. We later found out that they were using an old abandoned piece of land that was once a farmhouse, to store and hide their private planes.

Menna sweetheart, it is finally over, David said gently as he kissed Menna. You see Menna; the Fathers' Alliance has been part of the Mayors Task Force for many years now.

Colette's' wedding was beautiful. The Mayor was in attendance, along with the Fathers' Alliance. (Mayors' Task Force.) Collette is her old self again. She has some recollection of her past. She still remembers her sons' tragic death. Maybe Collette felt that she had to square herself with God. I guess this is how she did it. Even-though it won't bring her son back, maybe it will lessen her pain.

Collette still thinks about her son.

As for our city, the city of Buffalo has become a household word. Worldwide our city earned notoriety and publicity. Funding that you would not believe. Jobs and economy are high up on the ladder. Our city has become a major tourist attraction.

We now have a computerized satellite home office. This office handles top-secret data via the Federal government.

I guess that good does supercede evil. Goodness is a pre-requisite for life. Our city holds the proof.

Our deepest thanks go out to the city of Buffalo.

BUFFALO, MY HOME

Buffalo is my home
A place of care and concern,
Where the children's laughter can
Always be heard,
A feel of song and dance in the air,
Let everyone know we care,
A family that is what we are Always near, yet never far. A problem is a problem, we all pitch In and solve, an atmosphere of love Which knows no bounds.

The lives we lead are simple ones, But rich we know we are by far, As the sun comes down and glistens, On our storybook winter wonderland, That is the time we all know What a glorious city we live in A city called Buffalo.

THE END

"A NEW BEGINNING"

Mommy, I want to play with the ball. Said Mark. As he grabbed Mennas' stomach; no my ball argued Rachael. Children, said Menna, lets' get dressed so we can go see grandma and grandpa, said Menna. Mommy when is the baby coming, asked Rachael? Rachael, dear Rachael, said Menna "in about a month, replied

Menna.

Mommy, when is daddy coming hoe, said Rachael? Daddy will be home in three days children, for the weekend, from the base. Now children, said Menna, I have an errand to run, so speed it up before we are all late, said Menna. Mommy asked Mark can I take Pugsley to grandma and grandpas house? Leave Pugsley here Mark. Said Menna. Mommy, Mark has Pugsley in his pocket, said Rachael. Now Mark, said Menna what did I say? Mommy, said Mark this is my ninja turtle. "Mark give it to me, said Menna. Mommy, Pugsley looks just like Donatello, and we all laughed aloud.

As the children and Menna got into the car; Menna said, alright Kids, lets' put our seatbelts on, alright kids we are on our way to the grandparents house, said Menna; Yea, shouted Mark and Rachael as we were pulling out of the parking lot. Menna pointed out to the children what the street signs meant and the street light colors; Menna told the children, that she would be to there grandparents house to pick them up at 8:30p,m,;kids remember, said Menna, be nice to your grandparents, The children were going to the zoo with their grandparents, and later having a cookout.

Menna pulled into her parents driveway; Menna and David, and the kids had previously purchased. matching grandparents rings for our parents. with the childrens

Birthstones intact. Menna was delivering the rings. Menna rang the bell, it wasn't long before her parents opened the door, hi mom, hi dad, said Menna, here is something for you from us with love. Thanks dear, said mom and dad as they hugged Menna; You are welcomed. Replied Menna as she headed for the exit door, okay kids, said Menna, I have to go now, Menna kissed the kids and left.

As Menna pulled out of the driveway, she wondered how Anna was doing, she hadn't heard from or seen Anna in about a year; and today Anna was going to be discharged from the sanitarium. Anna had relocated back here, (Buffalo); Anna chose to live in an elegant security building., located in a more quiet part of town. Anna had no children, Anna was going back to work as a reported, that Tuesday Menna was to help Anna move into her new apartment.

As Menna pulled into the parking lot of the Pine Meadows rest home, Menna prayed that things would work out for Anna, Anna had a hard time taking the death of her husband. Annas' husband, Marshall was in law enforcement and he died in the line of duty. I pray that Anna can go on with her life now, it has been three years since the death of her husband.

REFLECTIONS OF LIFE

Menna made her way up to Annas' room, knocking lightly on the door. Anna was so excited about leaving the rest home; Looking at Anna, Menna could not believe the transformation from a year ago, Anna was Anna again.

As Menna helped Anna pack to leave, there was a tapping on the door, Anna answered the door and introduced Menna to a handsome young man, who was a doctor on staff, there at the rest home, his name was Jerrold Guyton; Hello, said Anna to Jerrod as Jerrold gently pecked Annas' cheek with a tender kiss. Hello, said Menna as she cleared her throat, I am going to go and Check Anna out, and Anna and I will meet you in the lobby. I see that you have all the help you nee, said Menna. Anna did not even answer, her and Jerrod just stood there affixed to their spots, looking at one another.

Well there isn't much to describing Jerrod, he was a very tall man, maybe six feet, he had dark hair, was kind've linky, in an Ichabod Crane sort of way, and was a very handsome and solemn acting sort of man. He reminded me a lot of Annas' husband.. (deceased).

On the drive home the scenery was beautiful; Hello, Anna, Menna said rapping lightly on the dash of her vehicle, now give Anna, who is the item? Said Menna. Oh Jerrod, said Anna casually, we met at the rest home picnic; Jerrod is a widow who has two children, and he is trying to pick up the pieces of his life. We are good for each other, said Anna. How does life feel now Anna? Asked Menna. A little scary, a little exciting; things are clearer to me now, since I don't have the alcohol to dull my senses. I guess this is like taking my first step, said Anna. Do you think that you are ready for a relationship, so soon, asked Menna. Jerrod is just a friend, Menna, he is a good listener, I haven't thought of anything intimate as of yet; Oh, I see, said Menna. Well Anna here you are, your new home, said Menna as she pulled into the building parking lot..

The busboy met Menna and Anna at the car with a luggage carrier; the place was newly remodeled, the only thing that Anna needed was her clothes, Anna had sold her other belongings.

The apartment was beautiful; it looked like something out of a magazine; "How much is this going to cost you Anna, asked Menna; Oh about 2500.00 a month, replied Anna, I will do just fine; Stanley (Annas' husband), had a big insurance policy, and for the past six months, I have been working, as part of my rehabilitation; I have plenty money saved, the insurance covered my hospital stay.. Well, now that that is out of the way; "remember Anna, I am here for you, said Menna, and remember you are coming out this weekend. David will be home that weekend, maybe we can go and see that new play and dinner afterwards; will Jerrod be attending? Asked Menna. Of course, replied Anna. Menna and Anna embraced and said their goodbyes Menna turned to leave, Anna watched Menn get into the elevator, the two waved goodbye and Menna was gone.

Menna looked at her watch; Oh dear, it is 7:30p.m., said Menna , where has the time gone; Menna headed to her parents ' home to pick up the children. As Menna put her key in the door she could hear the phone ringing, Menna went hurriedly inside, along with the children and answered the phone. "Hello, said Menna", Menna is this you< replied a voice on the other end of the phone? Tess, how are you, said Menna. Oh just fine replied Tess, I took some time off and you were on my mind, need I say more, said Tess. How is the shelter coming along, asked Menna; Good, said Tess, I am opening a second shelter in about three months, we are targeting troubled areas; I hears about your pregnancy, girl, said Tess, girl we have got about three months to catch up on everything. Tess, said Menna, the children and I are just getting in, let me ring you back, say 9:30ish, after the children are in bed. Better yet, said Tess, why don't I just stop through at that time to see you, I have something that I need to discuss with you; Okay Tess, said Menna, that will be fine.

Menna hung up the phone, she could not believe that she touched bases with Tess and Anna on the same day, what a wonderful surprise. Alright children, bathtime, said Menna as she put the bubble bath in the bath tub. Menna had the children in bed by 9:00p.m.; Mommy does angels have wings, asked Rachel, "They sure do, said Menna". Well, why don't I have wings, asked Rachel, you always call me your little angel. "That is because you are a different type of angel, you are a mommy angel, a mommy angel don't have wings, only a Gods' angel does."). I want to be a Gods' angel, said Mark, so that I can have wings. (Well Mark, said Menna, you will just have to settle for being a mommys' angel, said Menna, as she kissed the children goodnight. Menna outened the light and left the childrens room).

Menna sat out a dish of cinnamon rolls at 9:15p.m., and started a pot of coffee in anticipation of Tess. Tess was on time; still punctual as ever. Tess, Tess, Menna yelled, as she threw open the door. Menna, said Tess as they embraced and started to jump up and down like two school girls, come in Tess, said Menna. Menna and Tess sat down to a cup of coffee. Menna, said Tess, we have to move the location of the shelter, because the occupants have been turning up missing,. It seems like every week an occupant turns up missing, there is an investigation underway, so we have to move the shelter for a while. After this is cleared up, I will possibly keep the second center open.

My God, Tess, said Menna, what on earth is going on? I only wish I knew said Tess. Look at me Tess, said Menna, I am over eight months pregnant, there isn't much I can offer you in the way of help. I know that, replied Tess, just lending me your ear is help enough.

All I know, said Tess, is about a month ago, strange things started occurring, crank phone calls, power outages, vandalism to the building, on each occasion the police were notified. The women take turns going out to do the shopping, and to pay the bills., on or about August 7th one of the mothers' went to do the shopping and never returned.

That following week, we sent women out in groups of two, they also never returned, said Tess, this is really frightening, no leads have been reported since those disappearances.

I am sure everything will be alright, said Menna. I certainly hope so, said Tess, we have these womens' children to think about. Well, Menna, said Tess' I had better be going now, I am going to be staying with my folks for the next couple of months; Just until the new center opens up. Tess, said Menna, do you still have your home in the country? Yes, replied Tess, I was living there until these disappearances started happening. I don't know, said Tess, maybe I will sell the house and look for something smaller. Since Terry is away at school, the place just seems so empty. Well, replied Menna, I hope that you find something soon. I am in no hurry, said Tess; Well keep me posted, said Menna as Tess made her way out of the door; Will do, said Tess, Menna lets' have lunch next week, I will give you a call. Sure replied Menna. Menna closed the door and checked the locks, that conversation with Tess had made Menna a little jumpy.

Menna headed for the shower, (boy am I tired, said Menna to herself), as Menna turned on the water for her shower, she senses a presence in the room, she could feel the warmth, Menna began to shudder. Who is there said Menna.? Menna stood very still, for about ten minutes, until she felt the presence lift from her. Menna turned on the shower and did not think about the occurrence again. By 12:15 Menna was in bed and fast asleep.

As the week dragged on, the children were more peaceful than usual; we spent a lot of time at the park that week, letting the kids run off some of that energy; where do they get it from. Menna asked herself. The children were to stay the night at their grandparents ; they had plans ti see the play "Peter Pan", that afternoon.

That night Anna and Menna; David and Jerrod, were going to see the play "Sisters In the Name of Love" and out to dinner afterwards: David should be arriving at 1:00p.m., today The children are going to their grandparents home, via David. (the childrens father).

Thursday morning the children and Menna cleaned from top to bottom; There was no reason to rush, Menna told the children, we have plenty of time; The children and Menna made caramel suckers and baked cookies. (Menna did the caramel suckers, she did not want the children near that hot stuff). Menna also finished her preserves; Thursday was a fun day, that Menna and the children spent together.

Children it is 10:00a.m., said Menna, lets get dressed and go to the supermarket. Hurry, along children, said Menna, time waits for no one. Rachel, get your brush and comb, how many pig tails are you wearing today? I want two, replied Rachel, as she handed Menna her brush and comb. Okay, mommys' little angel, all done; Lets' see your teeth Mark. Did you clean your ears out real good? Yes, mommy, replied Mark; Okay, my little boy angel, lets' get going; Oh wait a minute kids, said Menna, let me get your overnight bag for granma and granpas house. I might as well put them in the trunk of the car. Okay kids you have toothbrushes at your grandparents house already.

Okay , now, I think that we have everything: Well lets' go to the market, said Menna. Menna did her shopping for the week; finally the three of them trooped to the checkout; The register rang up 132.00; my dear said Menna.

There must be some mistake. Menna and the children started to unload the shopping cart. Menna found the problem, it seemed that Mark and Rachael had done a little shopping of their own. Well, said Menna, I suppose I will have to write a check, since I only have about $82.00 with me. As Menna and the children pulled into the parking lot of the complex, They spotted David pulling in; Theres daddy yelled Mark and Rachael; "Wait , children yelled Menna, as they started to make a mad dash for their father. Children, said Menna, we do not run in a parking lot that way, we will meet daddy at the elevator, Menna yelled to David to meet them at the elevator. Menna and the children started to load the groceries out of the car. "Menna realized that they needed David to help with the bags, on second thought, David said Menna, we need your help, six bags of groceries, and there is only three of us , thought Menna. David came directly over; Hi honey, said David as he gently kissed Mennas' cheek, with a child in each arm; Hi, there said Menna flirtatiously. What have we here, said David; six whole bags, here you go Mark, a medium sized bag for you, a small bag for Rachael, and Menna you take the paper things, okay troops lets' hit it, David, said grabbing up the rest of the bags.

David and the children talked and played for about an hour; It was 12:45; time for the children to go to their grandparents home; Honey, take my car, said Menna, the childrens' overnight bags are in the trunk of the car. Some things that they will need for their grandparents home; Will do, said David, come here Mark and Rachael, said Menna, come and give me a hug, the children zipped their windbreakers and ran over to Menna, the three of them embraced, now children, said Menna please be nice to your grandparents. Yes mommy, said the children. Mom and dad will be bringing you home at 7:00p.m. and they will be visiting till 9:00p,m; See you then said Menna, the children were going to Davids' parents home this time.

Now for the hard part, said Menna, looking for something to wear. Menna went through her wardrobe and pulled out a two piece sequins skirt and top, oh, this will do, said Menna. Menna had washed and set her hair when the phone rang; Hello, said Menna; Hi, Menna, this is Anna; Anna, said Menna, you sound strange, is anything the matter? No, said Anna; I was just calling to let you know that Jerrod and me will be there promptly at 7:30, we have dinner reservations for 10:30, the curtain will go up at about 8:20p.m, so be ready. Okay, said Menna. Menna put the phone back into its' cradle My, thought Menna, Annas' speech was slurred, maybe its' nothing, said Menna as she let the thought leave her head.

At 4:00 p.m. David walked in the door; we made love and showered; David, said Menn, Tess was here to visit me Wednesday…as Menna filled David in as to what was going on , she watched David shake his head in disbelief. Did you notify the authorities and the Fathers' Against Violence on this asked David? Yes dear, replied Menna, but Tess is taking this pretty hard; I understand, honey, said David, I am sure that things will be alright alright; Any suspects, asked David? Not yet, said Menna; The missing women have not yet been found; Well Menn, these things take time, said David, why don't we say a little prayer for Tess, David suggested. As David and Menna joined hands, they began to pray; God said Menna we have encountered another problem, mommies are turning up missing; we have numerous children with no mommy. Please God, would you please take control of this situation; Please send those missing mommies home. Amen, said David, and Menna. Well dear, said David that is about all that we can do; I suppose you are right, replied Menna; Well David, it is now 6:oopm, why don't we watch the news. Body found in dumpster, of a woman, no positive identification has yet been made. Relax, Menna, said David; we have to hope for the best.

Now shouldn't we be getting ready for our night out; said David. I suppose you are right, said Menna, as she started to take the curlers out of her hair.

Jerrod and Anna, were on time, we invited them in for a quick non-alcoholic martini. I will drive said Menna as she mixed martinis, half alcohol and half non alcohol, I will have tomato juice anyway said Anna. Well, gang, said David lets' get going, curtain goes up promptly in less than 45 minutes While David and Jerrod were getting acquainted, Menna stared at Anna, Annas' eyes looked glazed, Menna could have sworn that Anna had been drinking, but she could not smell alcohol; Annas' speech was slurred, Anna, said Menna we will talk later, sure kid, said Anna. The valet, parked the car and the two couples walked into the theater, and were ushered to their seats. Later at the restaurant and night club, we dined on filet mignon, and danced to the soft soothing music. Menna felt a sharp pain to her abdomen at that moment . This can't be said Menna, it is to early. The pains began to come more rapidly and harder. David, said Menna, I think it is time to go to the hospital; David ushered Menna over to a chair at their table. Anna called the hospital, the valet hurriedly pulled the car up to the frontside of the restaurant, and then they were on their way to the hospital. David and Menna did the breathing together , Menna was taken immediately to the labor wing of the hospital. The pains were excruciating, like several blows to the stomach; David was in tears at the pain that Menna was enduring, finally, about four hours later, David and Menna were blessed with twins; two eight pound baby boys. Menna did not remember much after that, she just drifted off to sleep. Menna woke up in the recovery room. David was asleep in a rocking chair next to the bed that Menna was in.

Menna drifted off to sleep again, she dreamed of Irma, Menna dreamed that Gerald was in a sanitarium. Menna woke up covered in sweat; David, yelled, Menna, as he woke up. Menna burst into tears. Sweetheart what is the matter asked David.Its' Irma, Irma is in trouble, David please, a phone. I have got to call Irma. David handed Menna the phone, Menna looked for Irmas' phone number, flipping through the pages of her phone book. Menna dialed Irmas' number via long distance. Menna could not get through, the operator said the phone was disconnected. Menna, now, you have to calm down, you are to upset, as soon as you are better we will take a six hour drive to see Irma. I have taken an extended leave from my post, and I will be home for a while. Sweetheart, said David to Menna, you know that big gray and white house that you loved so much, the house that you picked out about three months ago? Well, it is yours, David said, as he handed Menna the keys. David, what? Squealed Menna; That's' right sweetheart, we closed Thursday. Via the base, I picked the keys up before I arrived home Friday; Here it is Menna and David Phillips; "David , you sneak, teased Menna. Now just relax sweetheart and everything will be alright. David, said Menna, I think it best that we call for a decorator, I think that would be best. Menna, said David, now I want you to rest. I will be back tomorrow; I will see if I can get permission to bring the children in to see their new little brothers. I will talk to our parents and give them the good news. I love you Menna baby, said David . I love you too David, said Menna, huskily as they kissed for at least five minutes, before they said goodbye. Menna watched David walk out the door and disappear down the corridor. Pictures of Irma kept shooting through Mennas' mind. Menna knew then that she would have to reach Irma.

On Mennas' first day home from the hospital, she didn't have any visitors, just her family; David, Mark, Rachel, and two sets of grandparents; Menna was to start interviewing housekeepers at 1:00p.m.. That day Menna interviewed eight housekeepers; she needed about a week to check references Menna was in her room resting; the grandparents were handling the children well.

Finally after two weeks, Menna found the perfect housekeeper, her name was Emma Thomas, a retired school teacher; Mrs Thomas was a widow , and a dear sweet woman; her hair was a silver gray; her skin was as smooth as silk, the richest bronze tone that Menna had ever seen. Mrs. Thomas was a jolly old woman, who was always in a hurry; and could light up a room with just a smile, and a kind word. Emma would be moving in, in about two weeks In that time Menna and her family would would be in their new home. Mrs. Thomas' references checked out and she had no criminal history; Mrs Thomas talked with an African accent, she was from Africa, and the children loved her.

FINALLY, THE MOVE: The move wasn't at all bad, Menna and David had hired movers; Moving is easier than I thought, said Menn, to herself. Menna could take some time off from work if she preferred; I suppose a couple of years to be home with the children; Menna had done well in an investment that she had made via her brother, who was an inventor. Menna had invested in three of his inventions, Menna nd her family could live comfortably off her royalties.. Menna was also a writer, so a few years would not really hurt. David was an army captain, and had invested in property.

Menna and David named the twins: Matthew, and Chad; The boys were really no trouble, with the help of Mrs. Thomas. Mark and Rachel were really excited about their new little baby brothers; Menna had Mark and Rachels' bedrooms remodeled. Rachels' room was done in a ice pink background, with fairy tale characters all over the walls. Marks' room was done in a midnight blue with red, yellow and ice blue sail boats all over the wall. Menna made matching curtains and bedspreads for each child' room

Our new home had four large bedrooms and two baths, with a large basement, which had been changed into a recreation room. This was our first home and we loved it; The nursery was a purplish blue with Sesame Street as the theme, the decorators did a beautiful job. When the children and Emma came in from the grocery store, at the same time the phone rang; Menna had just put the twins down for a nap. Drats, said Menna, quiet time gone. Menna answered the phone, hello, said Menna; Hi, Menna this is Tess, listen , I have to go over to the first shelter to collect some things, do you think that you could escort me in your van? Sure, replied Menna, perfect timing , I will be there in about thirty minutes. Good, said Tess. As Menna kissed the children , Menna said, Emma, I have an errand to run, you have my pager and cell phone number, call me if you need to. It is 2:00p.m. now I will try to be back in time for the childrens' bedtime story, and the twins feeding; Okay dear, replied Mrs. Thomas, as Menna hurried herself out the door.. A feeling of despair hit Menna: I might as well check on Anna, said Menna. I haven't heard from her in days. Menna pulled up in Tess' parents' driveway and blew the horn; Tess came right out.

Hey girl, what's' cooking said Tess. Oh nothing girl, replied Menna, I need to go and check on Anna, after we leave the shelter, lets' drive up and see her; "Sure replied Tess; I have been trying to reach Anna for days, but there is no answer; and she hasn't picked up her voice mail. Tess, said Menna do you feel that? Feel what, asked Tess. That eerie feeling, its in the air, what can it be, said Menna, Maybe its' just me, said Menna. I sure was relieved that the womans body found in that dumpster wasn't someone I knew, said Tess. I know what you mean, said Menna. Menna pulled up into the shelter parking lot. Tess noticed a van pulling off. Who can that be, said Tess we will never know, replied Menna.

Tess went to put the key into the door, but the door was already opened; (Now I know I locked it said Tess). Tess walked into the shelter, Tess told Menna that she was going upstairs to collect some things. Menna you can start packing up the software; Will do, replied Menna. I will be checking windows also, said Tess, just to make sure they are locked, so if you hear the alarm bell it is me, said Tess. Tess started up the stairs with a flashlight, that eerie feeling swept over Menna again. It must be Anna said Menna to herself, Menna continued packing up computer discs. All of a sudden , Menna heard a loud piercing scream coming from upstairs; Tess, oh my God Tess, yelled Menna as she ran upstairs; It was then that Menna saw it; A woman beaten and tied to the bed, her head was sitting on the pillow opposite her body, with a number 1 carved into her abdomen. Oh dear God yelled Menna, as she opened the closet door and looked in with the flashlight. Tess just stood there terror stricken. Tess, said Menna, softly shaking her; (no reaction; Menna let me go screamed Tess, fighting Menna as if she were the killer; Menna slapped Tess; Tess began babbling. Menna this is one of the women who has been missing from the shelter, the first missing woman;; Joanne Steverson; (Tess we had better wait for the police; Lets' go outside Tess, said Menna). The two walked quietly down the stairs, and out the door to Mennas' van.

When the police finally did arrive, Tess and Menna went over every detail with the police as they stood outside Mennas' van. On searching the rest of the house, the police found missing fingers and toes of the disfigured young women.Tess was so hysterical as we left the shelter, Menna felt that she should take Tess to the hospital for a sedative, and return her to her mothers' house. On the drive home, Tess was not responsive to conversation, Tess' mother helped me to get Tess into bed; Menna let Tess mom know that she would be back the following evening. It was about 4:00p.m. Menna needed to go home and check in and spend some time with her family before she checked Anna. Oh dear, said Menna this is a real shocker; the way w found Mrs. Steverson, is exactly the way Menna had found Tess some years before. I wonder if there is any connection, said Menna aloud to herself While nearing the driveway, Menna blew the horn and went directly inside. The children were happy to see Menna; Mommy, yelled Mark and Rachel, as they gave Menna a huge bear hug. Menna thought I had better not talk to Mrs. Thomas about this , it may upset her;. Menna went to check Matthew and Chad, they were asleep. Menna said good, I made it back in time for their feeding. Menna and Rachel began to toss the salad for dinner, while Emma prepared pecan pie for dessert. By 4:45 the twins (Matthew and Chad) were yelling to be fed. Menna checked the steaks, and she and Rachel went in to feed and diaper the twins. Twenty minutes later the twins were asleep again. (5:45p.m., just in time for dinner. Just as Mark, Menna and Rachel sat down for dinner the phone rang. Hello, said Menna, (Menna this is Irma.) . Irma I am sorry, this weekend I will be up there to visit you, David and I had planned to make the trip. (Good, replied Irma, I really need to talk to you). Irma I can't talk now, said Menna, but I will be there at

1:00p.m.; look for me, are you alright? Asked Menna. I don't know said Irma. We will talk, see you then, said Irma. As Menna hung up the phone, she asked herself, what could be wrong with Irma?

Mark had turned ten years old; and Rachel was seven; It was Mark who said mommy, are you to busy for Rachel and me? Of course not, said Menna; whatever gave you that idea> I don't know, said Mark. Well sweetheart you just remove that thought from your head. Yes mommy said Mark and Rachel. Well next weekend you and me and daddy will spend the whole weekend together at the base away from everything; What about Matthew and Chad? The babies will stay here with Mrs. Thomas. They are to young to travel yet; Grandma will be staying the weekend to lend Mrs. Thomas a hand. No wchildren, I have to see Anna, I will be home to read your story and tuck you in. Mark, Rachel, I love you' said Menna, hugging them both. Menna grabbed her blazer jacket, gave Mrs. Thomas a few details and was out of the door. Rush, rush is my life thought Menna to herself. Menna got into the van, she took a few minutes to open her mail. The telephone bill was almost 300.00, Mark and Rachel had been calling their dad at the base often by the looks of things. Well thought Menna, I will have to talk to the children. As Menna pulled out of the driveway, her thoughts flashed back to Anna. Anna won't answer her phone or return any of my calls. What is wrong with Anna now . It was a one hour drive to Annas' as Menna pulled into the parking lot, her heart started to race, something just wasn't right.

Children called Emma; Your mother want you to do your homework; shall we get started? Asked Mrs. Thomas. Yes replied Mark and Rachel: Okay children shall we be seated at the dining room table? The children and Mrs. Thomas seated themselves around a huge bowl of fresh popped corn; As Mark and Rachel complained (why do we have to do homework anyway, homework is so boring). Well, said Mrs. Thomas homework will help you to do well in school. Do your homework and afterwards we can go down to the rec room and play the Triple Arcade game, how about that? Yeah replied Mark and Rachel, as they handed Mrs. Thomas their work. Very good Mrs. Thomas, said as she posted a star on the chart next to Mark and Rachels' name. Children, put away your books, it is time to go to the rec room. Mrs. Thomas, set the alarm and gathered up the babies, and the five headed down to the rec room. Mrs. Thomas unloaded Chad and Matthew and put the two babies in the playpen; Then. she went over to Mark and Rachel, and turned on the video game. The children became engrossed in a game of pin ball; Okay, children, said Mrs. Thomas softly, 45 minutes till bath time.

Mrs. Thomas took out her knitting needles and started working on sweaters that she was making for the children. Okay children; it is time to pack it in now, said Mrs. Thomas, as she put her knitting away. Mrs. Thomas, can we have a popsicle? Asked Mark.. After your bath, said Mrs. Thomas. Yes mam, replied Mark, as he turned on his bath, and put just the right amount of Mr. Bubble into his water. Mrs. Thomas helped Rachel with her bath; but, Rachel was able to bathe herself properly. Well kids lets' settle down, we are going to watch a movie about Africa; until mommy gets home, to read you your story and tuck you in; Mrs Thomas said, as she handed the children a popsicle and turned on the monitor, and the movie. Mark and Rachel looked on in awe.

Mrs. Thomas went to check the twins, making sure that the monitors were on, she hurried to the twins room, checked the monitors one last time and scurried to the kitchen to do the dinner dishes. It was just 7:oop.m. thought Mrs. Thomas, and all is well. After tidying up and pulling back the childrens beds, Mrs Thomas joined the children, sitting in a rocking chair she had purchased, Mrs. Thomas continued with her knitting.

Everynight, Mrs Thomas was in bed and fast asleep by 10:oop.m.; and every morning Mrs. Thomas was up and showered, and dressed by 5:30a.m. Mrs. Thomas was really a dear woman, really a blessing.

Menna picked up her car phone and called home to check in with Mrs. Thomas. Hi, Emma: Are things alright? Yes, Mrs. Phillips, the children are waiting up for you to tuck them in and read them their story. Okay, Emma; It is now 7:20p.m., If I cannot be there, I will call the children, will that be alright? Yes, Mrs. Phillips; Okay Emma; see you soon. Nite, Ms, said Emma.

Menna rode up to Annas' apartment, and rung the bell, Menna heard loud noises behind the door; as if things were being thrown. Menna knocked harder on the door calling Annas' name, Menna turned the door knob to see if the door was unlocked, the door was unlocked. Menna went in, towards Annas' room, where the noise was coming from, Menna caught sight of Anna, standing in her bed, and throwing things, the place looked like a tornado had hit. Anna what is your problem, asked Menna? Menna noticed a half filled bottle of pills next to Annas' bed; Menna picked up the bottle, and read valium 10mgs. So that's' it said Menna to herself.

Anna, how many of these have you taken today? Said Menna. Anna get down off that bed. (Stay away from me, screamed Anna.). Menna checked the windows, Menna walked over to Anna and held out her hand to her. Anna just kept screaming and throwing things, Menna locked Anna in her room and went to telephone Jerrod. Jerrod knew of Annas' dependency to the tranquilizers he said that he knew that it had been going on for quite sometime; Anna had been going to at least three doctors, and getting the same prescription. Well what shall we do now, asked Menna? There is not a whole lot that we can do, said Jerrod; Anna is going to have to go through withdrawal, I will stay home with her, if she can get through this night, she should be okay. I took all of the medication that I could find that was laying around, but Anna still managed to find a hidden bottle of the pills. It is up to Anna. Relax, Menna said Jerrod, why don't you go home; you can talk to Anna tomorrow; There is nothing you can do tonight.

Menna looked in on Anna, who was asleep, Menna rubbed Annas' forehead and kissed her before she left. Outside Annas' door, Menna leaned up against the door and took a deep breath; Dear God Anna, what have you done to yourself now, Menna said to herself. Menna dragged herself to her van, she felt a feeling of defeat. Menna put her head back against the headrest of her van and looked upward toward the heavens; "God, said Menna, I guess by now you know what is going on with Tess and Anna, I know that we are far from perfect, as far as life is concerned. I just need to ask you dear God to please give me the strength to pull through, I ask that you see me successfully through these encounters with your adversary, the devil. You know God, I understand that you won't let Satan put no more on us than we can bear, who am I to question you. I ask you to give me the strength that I need, to guide and direct me in my every move. I love you my heavenly Father. Amen. Time to go home Menna, said a voice from out of nowhere. Menna pulled out into traffic and headed home at 8:30 p.m

Menna arrived home by 9:15pm. Menna went in, the children were on their way to sleep. Hi Emma, said Menna, as she walked over to her two sleeping children on the oversized sofa. How did things go today, asked Emma? Just fine, said Menna, "You look tired, said Emma; Dear, said Emma we only live once, whatever you do be sure to take your time, this allows room to immediately correct errors, save time and do it right, give your brain a chance to register. Thank you Emma said Menna, I guess in the back of my mind, I knew that, but I never realized how important it really was until now, you are a gem.

Menna picked up Rachel, and walked Mark to bed, Emma gathered up her knitting and started on her way to bed . The phone rang, hello, said Emma, the Phillips residence. Emma before I talk to Menna, I called to verify our lunch date for tomorrow, said Eloise. Mennas' mom, tomorrow is our outing day (Wednesday). Of course Eloise, replied Emma. You can pick me up along with the children at 11:30am, we will be ready. Okay ,

Emma replied Eloise, put Menna on the phone. Hello mother, said Menna, just to remind you dear, about our lunch date, I think I will keep Mark and Rachel for the day, I enjoy the company, sure mom. Emma will be attending too, said Eloise(Mennas' mom), so you can have a relaxing day. Yes mother, replied Menna. Nite dear said mom; nite mom, said Menna, love you mom, said Menna before she put the receiver back into its' cradle.

Menna went to the childrens' room and turned on the nite lights, she checked the monitors. Menna kissed the children and said a prayer for them. Menna made her way to the twins room; The boys were asleep. The boys would be waking up for the last feeding of the night, in about a half hour, Menna began preparing bottles and preparing diaper changes. Menna found a soft, soothing song to listen to. Menna picked something by Whitney Houston.

The twins woke up like clock work by 10:20p.m. Menna diapered the boys and used their car seats and bottle harnesses to feed them. Menna looked into their eyes and began singing along with the melodic voice on the CD player. The boys were wide eyed and looking on as if they were realizing, this is home. Menna enjoyed the boys for at least twenty minutes, before they drifted off to sleep. Menna quietly put the kids back to bed, after changing their bed pads, kissing their two little noses, checking monitors, night lights, and windows. Menna headed for the shower. Boy it feels good to be home, said Menna to herself. David will be home this weekend this weekend. Menna so needed to be close to her husband. Just two more days before Friday. After showering, Menna turned on the answering machine and made herself a cup of warm milk to help her to relax.

As Menna sat curled up on the couch, thoughts of Tess entered her mind. Menna would be going to take Tess to see her therapist at 2:00pm, that following day, Thursday. Tess was really taking these last chain of events bad, Tess barely left her mothers' side, her appetite was poor and Tess was having trouble sleeping. Tess' father had passed on, he gave his life for his country. Thank God that Tess has a loving mother to rely on. Menna drifted off to sleep on that oversized sofa, she dreaded going to bed without David. Many nights Menna fell asleep on that sofa, on awakening Menna always found herself covered up, with a blanket, and the television was always off, compliments of Emma.

That Thursday morning Menna awakened to the smell of fresh baked bisquits and coffee; God, must have been helping Menna out; Menna was always able to wake and shower before the twins woke up at 8am, its' like her head kept a silent alarm set for 7am. Mark and Rachel never woke up till 9am, by that time the twins were asleep again. Good morning Emma, said Menna. Good morning Ms, replied Emma; Eggs Ms., no thanks Emma, coffee is just fine.

Menna went to shower and get ready for the twins. That Friday Menna, David, and Mark and Rachel were going up to see Irma. Irma lived in Ontario, Menna looked forward to the long drive , and seeing Irma again. Today was Thursday, thought Menna, I had better check Anna after seeing after Tess, I will then pack some much needed things for the trip. Menna finally made it through the morning with the twins, Mark and Rachel. By 10:30, the children were settled and playing in their play room with building blocks ; Menna took the opportunity to get herself dressed, Emma should be back by 1:00p.m from her outing with the children and mom. Menna checked the twins, who were still sleeping. Menna worked with Mark and Rachel and fingerpaints until mom arrived. Mom arrived at 11:45 and Emma, Mark and Rachel were on their way. Emma returned home at 1:15pm. Emma said Menna, the twins are sleeping and I should be back no later than 4 pm.

Menna wondered on her drive to Tess' house, had any leads turned up since that tragic event. Menna pulled in to Tess' moms' driveway. Menna rang the bell and Tess' mom let Menna in. Hello Mrs. Gibbs (Tess' mother), how is Tess doing these days? Asked Menna. Not to good these days, replied Mrs. Gibbs, Tess is not as outgoing as she once was. Tess is not the conversationalist that she used to be. I pray that this therapist can help her; He comes highly recommended. Who is he, asked Menna, his name is Dr. Ignatius Weber. Oh yes, said Menna, I have heard of him; Oh by the way Menna, said Mrs. Gibbs; Do you think that you could take Tess' car, and park yours, Tess, car has been sitting there for weeks now, it would be a shame to let a perfectly good car just go to waste, sure Mrs. Gibbs, replied Menna Tess owned a beautiful yellow, Stingray. Mrs. Gibbs called up for Tess' to come down from her room.. Before Tess and Menna left for Tess' appointment, Mrs Gibbs gave Menna a card with the doctors, name and phone name, address, and phone number on it...

Tess and Menna headed for Tess' car,. Tess said Menna , why is the trunk opened, Menna walked over to the trunk to close the door of the compact trunk. The trunk was more deep than wide, Tess followed in a trance like state. Menna tried to close the trunk, but it seemed as if something was preventing the trunk door from closing. Menna opened the trunk, as Tess stared into the air. On glancing at the contents of the trunk, Menna began to gag, finally throwing up. Tess screamed at the top of her lungs, There in the trunk of Tess' car was a clear plastic bag, with a womans body inside. The womans' extremities were separated from her body. The woman was decapitated. Menna ran to her car and started to blowing the horn, frantically; her heart was racing so fast, that Menna thought that she would have a heart attack Menna grabbed for her car phone and dialed the police, Menna also requested an ambulance.

Menna ran over to Tess and grabbed her and held her to keep Tess from shivering Menna said Tess stop and come out of the garage, Tess come with me, said Menna. Tess started fighting Menna, yelling for Menna to get away from her. Menna slapped Tess to quiet her down, Tess just automatically relaxed, tears started streaming down Tess' face, Menna why, why, asked Tess God Tess, I don't know. Menna felt as if she was going to lose it. Finally the police arrived and an ambulance, a statement was taken. The police were at that crime scene for hours. Menna phoned Tess' therapist to meet them at the County Hospital. Mrs. Gibbs and Menna rode to the hospital with Tess, Menna took her own vehicle. Menna phoned home to let Emma know that she would be late; Tess was admitted into the hospital for evaluation. The detective working on the case was the same officer who answered the call years ago when Tess was in trouble. Tess was on twenty=four hour guard at the hospital. Tess' mother informed us that Terry (Tess' daughter), would be here from Hillmon College to visit with and check on her mother. Terry would be arriving sometime Friday morning. Menna let Ida Gibbs (Tess mom), know that she would be going out of town for the weekend and would be back Monday morning , and that she would contact her then.

Would you like for me to take you home Mrs. Gibbs, asked Menna. No Menna, replied Mrs. Gibbs, I will be taking the room next door to Tess, so I will be here, the detective will be going home with me to pick up a few things, that we may need , you may call me here. Yes, Mrs. Gibbs, said Menna, I will call you Monday. Menna left the hospital and headed for Annas' house.

When Menna arrived to Annas' house, she found Anna in restraints, and Jerrod was there with her. Jerrod loved Anna; I knew that now. Anna was sleeping, Jerrod explained to Menna that the restraints were for Anna's protection, so that she couldn't hurt herself .Jerrod went on to let Menna know that Anna would be in the restraints, not more than twenty four additional hours. These last twenty four hours would be difficult for Anna, since she isn't allowed any medication whatsoever, getting Anna to eat and drink is not quite so easy, but Anna would be fine.

Menna went into Annas' room to visit with her, Menna sat down on the side of Annas' bed, Anna, said Menna, I am here, and I want you to know that I miss the way we were. Anna wasn't talking, she was just so angry. Anna , do you remember when Luther climbed the tree in our yard and could not get down? Remember we called the fire department, but Anna you could never stand to see to see Mark and Rachel sad, so you went into the house, and put on my sweats and sneakers and sneakers and you climbed that tree, you did not think about pain or danger you just did not want the children to be saddened. Three times, Anna, you started up that tree and you could not make it, finally the fourth try and you made it Anna, you climbed that tree and rescued Luther. That is when I realized that you were not weak, you were a fighter, and there was no obstacle that you could not overcome. Anna, I know you, Jerrod does not know you that way. Anna, you do not need restraints, you don't need this, Anna when I come back here Monday, I want my old Anna back, do you hear me Anna? Mennas' eyes started to fill with tears. Anna, you did it for attention, I will not feel sorry for you, you just can't keep taking time off to screw your life up, either you are going to do it right or just don't do it at all.

Anna, I will not do it anymore, you need to be standing with me and not on the other side, pulling in the opposite direction, Anna. Tess is in trouble and she needs our help, I need you Anna, you stop it right now. Jerrod ran in and stopped in his tracks. Do you hear me Anna, Menna yelled, tears streaming down her face. Jerrod ran over and held on to Menna. , Jerrod., let me go said Menna. Jerrod released Menna. Anna, call me, said Menna, I won't be back, you call me and let me know when you are ready to stand with me, I love you Anna, goodbye.

Menna ran to her car, and cried. God, said Menna, I did what you told me to do. Dear God it hurts. I remember the pain when Melody died. God it feels like that. I love Anna,   but Anna can't love me back if she doesn't love herself to care. God I don't have any magic words to make a bad life better, but I have you God to show me the way. I need a little strength so that I can endure these unhappy feelings. God would you mind seeing me through this one.   AMEN

Friday AM, David and Menna decide to go and check on Irma instead of our usual quiet weekend.

All packed and ready to go said Menna, as she loaded up the camper. Menna, called David. Yes honey, said Menna, did you remember to pack my shaver? No dear, said Menna you are using it. The children, David and Menna all started laughing hysterically, Mennas' mom would be there this weekend to help Emma out this weekend. The children said their goodbyes, to the twins; David and Menna left instructions with Emma before they all loaded into the camper.

REFLECTIONS OF LIFE

The Phillips family took the scenic route. The view was beautiful. Cows, horses, and rich green grass, was our view. The drive would last six hours it was by 4:00p.m that we figured we should be at Irmas'. Irma had asked us to stay with her and the children. Irma and Jerry lived in an old mansion that they had purchased after they relocated. Jerry was a teacher, and carpenter, and a college professor. In his spare time he bought antiques back to life, as he put it. Irma was a Pediatrician and had a doctors' office inside her home..

David honey, asked Menna would you like some coffee; I am going to put the children down for a nap, Sure honey said David. Menna went to the children, who were in the livingroom quarters of the camper. The children were half asleep already. Menna put the children to bed and prepared coffee for her and David. Menna, asked David, Ehat is it honey, replied Menna? Sweetheart, I think it best that you let the police handle the problems that they are involved in. What are you saying David, asked Menna? I am saying, that enough is enough. No more Menna, this is becoming to dangerous. David replied Menna, do you mean that I am suppose to let the people that I care about down. No Menna, said David, that is not what I mean, I just don't want you and the children any deeper involved than you already are. I don't want you and the children hurt, can you promise me that you will at least contact the Fathers' Alliance on extremely dangerous matters? Are you angry, David? No, Menna not angry just concerned for your safety. David, you know me, replied Menna. I remember when we were in college, after you achieved your degree, that still wasn't enough for you, David my hero, had to always be daring and live on the edge, so my dear David goes off to fight a war, leaving the children and me alone. I did not protest because I knew it was something that you just had to do. While you were away my friends were here for me. They pulled me through the emptiness that you left me with, and now you want me to choose between you and them, and just walk away from them, David I can't. Well, replied David, how about a compromise? Okay David said Menna I will notify the Fathers' Alliance. Promise me Menna, said David. I promise replied Menna. David let out a sigh of relief as we pulled into a rest stop area.

We finally made it to Ontario. David and Menna looked for Irmas' address, we thought it better to check out the situation before deciding whether to stay with Irma or not. We could always camp out. David had reserved a campsite for the children and myself. The campsite was about two miles from Irma. Menna and David decided not to take the children into the house right away. Menna waited in the camper and David went in to Irma.

David came back to the camper with a look of disbelief showing on his face.

David, what is wrong, asked Menna? Please go and talk to Irma, I will wait here with the children Menna stepped out of the camper and walked to Irmas 'door. Menna knocked on the door,, Irma yelled for Menna to come in, the door is open said Irma. Menna went inside Irmas' home

Menna noticed that Irmas' eyes looked red and tired, Irma had not done her nails. Irma was a stickler for manicured nails. That was Mennas' first time seeing Irmas' nails cracked and split with peeling polish. This took something away from Irma. Irmas' posture was drawn and bent looking, like all the fight had gone out of her, Mennas' eyes fell, she could not believe how so different Irma looked. Irmas' hair was pulled back into a ponytail, which it was evident that Irma did not take the time to do her hair. This was not at all like Irma. Irma seemed so withdrawn from the things around her. Irmas' children were at her mothers' house and had not been home for weeks.

Irmas' mansion was decorated beautifully, the wooden floors glistened even in the dark. Mahogany walls that you could see yourself in, the lighting was exquisite, with the beautiful chandeliers and paintings which complimented the mansion..

Hello Irma said Menna, how are you doing these days. Not so good, said Irma. An emergency came up with Gerald. I found Geralds' journals Menna it seems that Gerald has been practicing cannibalism, when I questioned him about it, three weeks ago, Gerald just left without a word. I often look out my bedroom window and I can see Gerald standing there in the shadows, but he won't come into the mansion. I believe that Gerald is coming in and out as I lay sleeping, I can feel him standing over me. There is another entrance that he is using, a trap door or something Gerald is acoiding me, so that he won't have to talk about it. Are you sure you have the facts straight, asked Menna? Are you sure that you are not drawing things out of proportion? Menna, just read this, replied Irma as she handed Menna one of Davids' journals. Turn the book to page five. Menna read page five and looked up at Irma in disbelief. It says that they drugged her and drained the blood out of the body before consuming it. But how do you know that Gerald is involved? Who is Gerald referring to, when he uses the word they? There are names mentioned, but no mention of Gerald, no mention that Gerald was a participant. Gerald is the third person, it seems as though he is telling a story. Irma did you contact the police about this, asked Menna. I notified the police about Geralds' strange behavior, the police are familiar with the journals. These journals date all the way back to before Gerald started teaching at the college, that was about two years ago.

Irma let me see what I can come up with, are you going to stay in this big old house by yourself. Asked Menna? Why don't you let me drive you to your mothers' house, you can stay with the children we can lock up the house and you can leave with us. I don't think that you need to be here alone. Maybe you can stay with Anna for a few daysor whatever you prefer. Irma made a call to her parents and decided to drive back with David , Menna and the children.

As we drove that long winding road, Menna could not help but notice how dark it was. David saw headlights of a blue pickup truck pull onto the road from out of nowhere, traveling very fast. David pulled over, and let the vehicle pass. The truck sat back on the road, about twenty-five feet from David, and just stood there, Menna made sure that everyone had their seatbelts on. David reassured the passengers that the camper had a lot of steel and power behind it and that everyone would be alright. David pulled back onto the road and noticed that the truck was following them. The truck stayed behind us all the way to Irmas' moms house. The driver did not get close enough for David and Menna to get a plate number. Once at home David noticed that the truck had tailed them all the way to there home. Menna had seen that truck before, but she just could not recall where once inside the safety of their home, Menna tried to recall the truck and where she had seen it before, but nothing seemed to click. Menna bathed and put the children to bed, sat with the twins; Matthew and Chad, for a while. Menna went to join David and Emma in the family room. How were the twins, asked Menna The twins were no trouble at all said Emma, and what time did momma go home, asked Menna. Oh about 8:00pm said Emma the four of us had a wonderful weekend. Well, said David as he stood up and started to stretch, I think I think that I will do some reading before I turn in. David turned and headed for the study, I am going to take a shower and turn in said Menna as she headed for the bathroom, see you in the morning, said Emma it is way past my bedtime.

Boy, am I tired said Menna as she toweled dry and headed for her bedroom. Menna climbed into bed and was asleep before she finished her prayers.

That morning Menna woke up to the cries of Chad and Matthew, wanting to be fed, Menna looked over at David who was still sleeping; It was 5:30am Menna said as she turned on the bottle warmer. Menna went to change the twins, when she noticed that Chads' genitals were swollen and disfigured. . Menna. woke David; out of sheer panic, David and Menna woke Emma and let her know what was going on, informing her that Menna and David would be taking Chad to the Childrens ' Hospital, and the doctor would be meeting them at the hospital.

As David and Menna drove to the hospital; Menna noticed that Chad was burning up with fever; Menna prayed that Chad would be alright; "Dear God, said Menna, a whole lot is going on right now; I ask you to give me the strength to endure what I cannot change; Please let little Chad be alright; he is so tiny, I hate to see him sick like he is now; be my strength and my guidance AMEN.

Menna and David found out after Chad was examined, that he had a hernia and would need surgery. The hernia comes from straining to come into the world ; After the surgery Chad should be fine; Chad would be hospitalized for three to five days; Menna stayed with Chad, that next day David was to leave for the base; Menna called Emma and her mother to let them know what was going on; Menna stayed that night at the hospital in a bed next to Chads'.

Chad, so tiny with those needles and tubes in him really saddened Menna; Menna sat in a rocking chair next to Chads' bed; The surgery was scheduled for the following morning; Menna dozed off and on all that night

That morning at 6am, Chad was taken to surgery; Menna waited in a waiting area; The surgery lasted for about an hour; After the surgery was over, the doctor came out and told Menna that things went well; Little Chad would have to remain in the hospital for another seventy-two hours. Those were the worst seventy-two hours of Mennas' life, Chad was finally allowed to go home and the welcoming committee was there; Mom and Dad, Mark Rachel, and Emma. Chad just slept. I do not think that Chad even saw his welcoming committee, he was just tired and all he did was sleep. Menna finally put Chad to bed and let the others know that she would be taking a nap; Menna napped for about forty five minutes, when the telephone rang, waking Menna up.It was Anna calling Menna; Anna needed to see Menna. Sure Anna, said Menna; Only, I cannot make it this week, something has come up with Chad . He had an operation, and I need to be here for him; If you need to see me sooner, said Menna, you are free to come to my home. How about Monday of next week, said Anna; After the children are bedded down? "Fine. Said Menna , say about 10:30pm. The two said their goodbyes, and Menna turned back over and drifted off to sleep.

It wasn't long before Mark and Rachel came into the room jumping up and down in Mennas' bed, yelling mommy, mommy we want to go to the park. It was about 2:45p.m., maybe some time in the park would help to clear my head. Thought Menna. Okay kids, just give me a few minutes; at that moment Emma came in to get the children: We want to go to the park, said Mark and Rachel to Emma. Its' okay, said Menna to Emma., maybe I need a walk in the park, the kids and I will be back in time for dinner. Said Menna.

What a beautiful day, thought Menna to herself as the children and Menna walked three blocks to the Roosevelt Park; Children, said Menna, I will be going back to work at school come Monday. I have to put on an art and fashion show that the Womens Writers Guild is sponsoring. Mommy, I thought that you were going to take off to be home with Chad and Matthew, said Mark, I know dear , said Menna. but I had planned the show last year. We need to raise money for the Childrens Shelter, said Menna. So this year I plan to work the remainder

Rachel ran over to the sand box and started to build her castle; Mark played on the exercise bars; both children were busy at play. Menna spread out a blanket. Menna thought about Tess; Menna had to take Tess to a doctors' appointment (therapist), Tuesday at 9am, I guess that a few hours from work won't make such a big difference, besides I am not scheduled to work this year. This time I am volunteering for a cause. Mark pay attention to what you are doing on those bars, Rachel don't put sand.

In your eyes by touching your face, you have sand on your hands, said Menna. The children played for about an hour before heading home.

That Monday was hectic; after being home those last three month; When arriving to school, Menna signed in and went to the office to check her message box. Hello Allan, said Menna, as she entered the office, can I help you, said Menna? Allan was a very bright eighth grader, Mrs. Phillips replied Allan: do you think this mural would be alright for the first floor hallway wall in the corridor? Allan handed Menna a beautiful oil painting; Why Allan it is beautiful said Menna. The painting was done in rainbow colors; with emphasis on the blues; It was beautiful.

Allan was really a model student; And his grandparents encouraged him, along with his mother. Allans' grades showed the support he received from home. The staff was very pleased with Allans' progress; I guess those homework sessions that the school offered. Really, paid off.

Allans' mother had heart trouble; And Allans' father was a decorated war hero. He lost his legs in the Vietnam War; Allans' dad was always there for Allan and his mom. He did not want to be a burden to his family with his affliction; So he thought it best he leave home. Allans' dads' mental state was not good. Of course his family wanted him home, but Allans dad never got over the loss of his limbs, so I guess Allan and his mom learned to accept his fathers decision Allan called Dr. Woods (principal); Yes, Dr. Woods, said Allan; :Don't forget your entry for the art competition which must be in by Friday, has to be officially entered. Today happens to be Tuesday: You have two days left; Yes, Dr. Woods, replied Allan, excitement showing in his face,

That was one of the many contests that Allan entered; Allans' mom needed an operation that could correct her heart condition The school had been taking donations, some of the children had collected money; Allans' mom was going to have her surgery, due to the childrens' efforts, as well as Allans' contest winnings.

That Friday came and all the contest entries were in; including Allans' That Monday, Dr. Woods met me at the teachers mailboxes with the news that Allans' mom had passed away during the night. That Saturday a.m., and that Allan would be out of school till further notice. Allan was in the care of his grandparents.

I think that I will go by and offer my condolences, said Menna to Dr. Woods. That is a good idea replied Dr. Woods. You can take the monies collected to the grandparents, they will be needing it now. I have a check in the amount of 1200.00, which is made out to the grandparents' of Allan. I will deliver the check, said Menna. Good replied Dr. Woods. My what a shock Menna thought, as she made the call to Allans' grandparents that night. Menna arranged to see Mr, and Mrs. Woods that Saturday afternoon.

The children were going to ride out to the base that morning with their father, to spend the day. They have a day when fathers bring children in for a picnic with all sorts of games and fun. Of course, moms are welcome, but it was mainly for fathers and their children.

On arrival to the Jones home; Menna noticed the grief that the house held; Menna saw Allan withdrawn; In his own little world. Menna tried speaking to Allan, but she did not think that Allan even saw her or heard her. The Jones were very solemn, but alert; they offered Menna refreshments, but Mennas' mind kept flashing to Alla, who was so disconnected from everybody else. Menna asked the Joneshow was Allan taking his mothers passing? Allans' grandparents replied that Allan hasn't cried or uttered a single word since he found his mother; He must have thought she was sleeping, because he had gotten himself ready for school, and didn't smell breakfast cooking. Allan must have went to check his mother, and found her that way. The school called us Friday at 10am, to tell us that Allan had not yet arrived to school that morning; He was suppose to be in school early that Friday to set up for the art exhibit. On calling Allans' house there was no answer; Pa and me went over to Patricias' house (Allans' mom). We kept a spare key, due to Pats' heart condition, said Mrs. Jones; We found

Allan laying on his mothers' chest; he hasn't spoken a word since he last recounted the incident. This morning, Allan just stopped talking at all. "Poor Allan, said Menna, he was doing so well."

Here is a check; The children have been taking donations; Trying to raise money for Patricia Cramden* , (Allans' mother) surgery, but now I guess you can find some other use for the money; I wish that it was something more that I could do, I wish the check could have been more, said Menna. Pleas accept my heartfelt sympathy, for such an untimely tragedy. Menna left her card with the Jones, and asked them to call her if there was anything that she could do. Menna headed back to work, she finally asked God to please pull that nice Jones family through such a terrible tragedy, and please God, do that special something for me. Allan he needs your help.

The funeral was full of grief-stricken people. However, everyone tried to maintain their composure during the service; Menna saw Allan with that expressionless look on his face, the Jones seemed to be in control. Menna left directly after the funeral and went to pick the kids up from school that Tuesday.

The children asked about Allan; Mommy where is Allan going to live now; Mommy did Allan cry; Mommy when is Allan coming back to school; Tons of questions that only children can ask. On arrival home the children and I settled down to our everyday routine; Homework, dinner, and a movie.

Finally it was bedtime, after tucking the children, in Menna settled down with a cup of tea and a good book. Menna really could not concentrate on reading her book. Mennas' mind drifted back to Allan and how hard he was taking his mothers' death; (time heals all wounds, said a voice).

Two weeks after Allans' mother had passed, Menna noticed that Allan had come back to school however, Allan did not look like Allan anymore. Allan had lost weight, his hair wasn't combed, he did not even bother to wash his face, his eyes were dazed. Menna never even saw Allan blink, his clothes were wrinkled as if he had slept in them. Menna walked up to Allan and asked him was anything the matter? Allan just shrugged his shoulders and hurried off to class.

Menna went to the office to phone Allans' grandparents. Menna asked the grandparents had Allan had any changes in his lifestyle since his mother' passing? Mr. And Mrs Jones informed Menna that Allan rarely stayed home anymore. His whereabouts are unknown; Sometimes,we do not see Allan for days at a time.

Has Allan been receiving any counseling, asked Menna? Allan does have numerous unkept appointments, informed, the Jones. It is almost as if Allan has just given up, said Mrs Jones, we cannot seem to reach him. We found drugs hidden in Allans' room, the day after the funeral, when pa and me questioned Allan, and got rid of the drugs, Allan became very upset and hostile, and left. Allan has not been back since. He comes and goes while we are sleeping, but he avoids us, its' like he doesn't want to face us.

Who is Allans' therapist? Asked Menna. Dr. A Carver: Located at 7225 East Meadowlane Street; the number is listed; Yes Mrs. Jones, we are familiar with Dr. Carver, he is a very good choice. Allan is in school today, he doesn't look to good, said Menna, I felt you should know. There is no need in coming in, let me talk to Allan and see if I can persuade him to come home and see a doctor, I will be in touch, said Menna,. Good Day Mrs. Jones, said Menna as she put the phone back into its' cradle.

Menna, checked Allans' schedule, Allan was in lunch now. Menna notified Dr. Woods as to the status of Allan and his condition. Menna made her way to the lunchroom. On arriving to the lunchroom, Menna scanned the tables and chairs for Allan. Menna spotted Allan laying his head atop the lunch table fast asleep. When the bell rang , Allan did not hear it, he remained sleeping. Menna escorted the children out, and returned to the lunchroom for Allan. Menna tried waking Allan, but Allan wouldn't wake up. Menna phoned for an ambulance. Something was terribly wrong, Menna notified Dr. Woods and escorted Allan to the hospital via her car. Allan had overdosed on amphetamines, but Allan would be alright. The ambulance arrived in just the nick of time. Dr. Woods notified Allans' grandparents.

Menna went to the hospital to visit Allan three days after the incident, however there was no trace of Allan. Allan had left the hospital, sometime during the night. Menna did not even get a chance to connect with Allan. Allan had to be found, he needed medical attention.

Menna returned to school, after letting Dr. Woods know what was going on, Menna contacted some friends of Allan'. It was really hard getting anything out of them. Menna explained to them, that thirteen year old, Allan was in grave danger that could cost him his life. We need to find Allan to arrange for medical attention for him. One of the girls stopped Menna as she turned to walk away. Mrs. Phillips, said the young lady, Allan is aat the Heartbreak Hotel.; The Heartbreak Hotel, said Menna, that place has been condemned for years, a lot of runaways frequent the place.

After school, Menna took the children to their grandparents' house and picked up two of Allans' close friends, they headed for that rundown place. When Menna and some of Allans' friends arrived there, they went inside, the children seemed to know the place well. On entering the run down place, Menna noticed well over fifty runaways hiding out in this place, called Heartbreak Hotel. Some of the girls were with child. Some even had children. The stench of the marijuana and urine was overpowering. There was no running water. One toddler was running around covered in fecal material. The children asked around (Allans' friends). Menna could not take her eyes off of the toddler. Menna asked who the baby belonged to, no one said a word. One kid came up to Menna and, said that she was tending the kid until the mother returned. You are just a kid yourself, I will take this baby with me, said Menna, taking the hand of the toddler. One of the teens informed Menna and the kids that Allan is in and out, he usually crashes here. Menna notified the police and the Mayors office, when she took the toddler to the police station. The Leutenient assisted Menna in making a call to the Mayors Office. Menna knew that these parents were looking for their children, some of these kids could not have been any more than ten years old. Once Menna and the kids left the place, Menna prayed; (God if one nation is but a drop in the bucket to you, then to ask you to save these children cannot be asking for to much; These gifts from you are killing themselves. You see this God, please don't be long in answering.   AMEN

Menna went back and picked up her children from their grandparents house, she felt at an all time low. Finally the children and Menna dragged through their usual routine, finally it was time for bed. Thank goodness, Menna said to herself, maybe tomorrow I will feel better.

About 2am, there was loud banging on Mennas' door, when Menna opened the door she saw Allan standing there. He was in a terrible state. Allan was on something, he did not look like himself, Allan was afraid and needed help. Allan was experiencing what the kids call a "bad trip".

Allan said to Menna, "help me, I don't feel good". Menna ushered Allan in: Allan asked Menna, what did you take? Menna picked up the phone and called for an ambulance. Allan replied, "I don't know Mrs. Phillips, someone slipped it to me". Menna phoned Allans' grandparents to let them know Allans' state. Menna phoned for Mrs. Clark, and the ambulance was there.

I don't know, said Menna, Allan got hold to some acid. I don't know if Allan will ever be Allan again, Allan is now withdrawn, he is not aware to what is going on around him anymore. Allan won the art show for the best exhibit, but he will never know. Allan is a vegetable now and so is his father.

Heartbreak Hotel is now a licensed home for runaways. For the life of me, I cannot understand, why did it take something like this? I guess people don't pay attention to themselves, like the bible tells us to do. If everyone would do that, then Allan would know that he won the art contest. Menna said God, I need a little more help, a little more strength to deal with the losses. God, it hurts to bad. There is still a chance that Allan will come around, but as of now maybe he just doesn't want to face the pain, the hurt. Maybe Allan is doing what Melody did. In a sense, maybe it is easier for Allan. I do not know, all I know is what I see when I focus on Allan now.

My a lot has happened in two weeks, said Menna as she pulled out of her driveway, heading for Tess' house (mothers'). Menna blew the horn before she went in. Menna went to the door, ringing the doorbell; Menna waited for someone to come to the door, Mrs. Gibbs, said Menna, how is Tess doing today? Tess has been in her room, since her release from the hospital. What about security, asked Menna? There are a few marked cars on the street, we are safe, I hope, said Mrs. Gibbs. Tess should be ready , come in Menna. Once inside the house, Menna went up to Tess' room. Tess was ready for her appointment. Menna escorted Tess to her car. Tess asked Menna, after my appointment, can we swing by the post office, I have to pick up my mail. Sure replied Menna, How is the treatment coming along? I won't know, said Tess, I was learning to deal with these things that frighten me. (Facing your fears is what they call it). Have you talked to Anna? asked Tess. Anna called me about two weeks ago, Anna was suppose to come and see me; however, Anna never showed up; I called her, but all I could get was her answering machine; I will have to go and see Anna, said Menna. Tess will you be free this afternoon? Asked Menna. Why what is going on asked Tess? I wanted to stop and check on one of my students. Would you like to come along? Besides you haven't even seen Irma in a while, said Menna. (Sure said Tess, I need the fresh air. After being cooped up so long it just might do me a bit of good,). As Menna and Tess pulled into the lot; Menna reached out for Tess' hand. Menna squeezed gently, and said, Tess continue to pray for strength>I have been praying, said Tess, I feel as if my prayers are being answered. I am starting to feel better about things. God does answer prayers.

Tess got out of the car and headed to her therapy appointment; Menna parked and went to the waiting room; Menna thumbed through the magazines, while waiting for Tess. Menna called home to let Emma know her schedule and to tell her that momma would be picking Mark and Rachel up from school today; So, don't worry, momma will call you. Okay ms, said Emma. Tess finally came out, about an hour later.

Tess and Menna headed for the Post Office ; Tess went in while

Menna waited in the car, Twenty minutes later, Tess appeared with a large box and plenty mail. Tess must have let her mail accumulate for quite sometime. My goodness, said Menna, as Tess climbed into the car; you can open your own post office. You said it girl, replied Tess

Since we have to go that way, lets' go and check my student first, his name is Allan. Allan lost his mother recently. His mom had a heart problem. Allan is about fourteen years old, a very bright student who is trying to cope with his problem. His dad is a vegetable, and a decorated war veteran.

Menna and Tess neared Allan' house, Tess decided to go in with her, since Tess had experience in dealing with troubled youths. Mr. And Mrs. Jones was very hospitable, as they ushered Tess and Menna indoors. The Jones' explained to Tess and Menna that Allan rarely comes home, he just hangs out there somewhere in those streets,Where does Allan usually go when he leaves here, asked Menna? He doesn't tell us anything. He just leaves. He doesn't even take the time to sit down and talk to us, said Mrs. Jones.

Okay, said Menna. I will be in touch. As Menna and Tess walked to Mennas' vehicle.. Menna noticed a car full of young men driving recklessly. Menna noticed Allan running through the alley, coming their way, heading towards home. The unknown car, cut Allan off and four young men jumped from the vehicle. Tess immediately ran over and stood next to Allan. Menna said Tess, the trick is to take an authoritive approach in dealing with teenagers, most, times they listen. We cannot be afraid of our children)

Tess immediately ran over and stood next to Allan. "We will have none of that, said Tess, shoving one of the boys. Menna walked over and took Allans' arm. Come on Allan, said Menna. Excuse me, said Menna, as she pushed through the crowd. You kids don't have anything better to do, than to try and hurt each other.? What is this all about anyway, said Menna.. (Lady, I don't have to tell you nothing, said one of the teens). Listen to me young man, before I stand out here and watch you go to blows, the four of you beating up one child, you will tell me something, and don't you talk back to me, Menna said, as she shoved him one good time, I am the adult not you. (Lady you had better go, before I forget you are a woman, said another one of the teens). Menna grabbed a stick that was lying on the ground next to a tree, and said, now you walk up on me. Menna raised the stick ready to use it, come on, said Menna, since you want to act like kids instead of young adults you will be treated as such. Tess stood in front of Allan. Menna yelled, now go, do you hear me go! Mennas eyes met theirs with anger, the kids sensed this and turned to leave. The boys yelled back to Allan; We want our money, you're lucky that your moms was there.. Allan bolted to run, Menna grabbed Allan, oh no you don't, said Menna, as Tess and Menna made Allan get into the car.

Now Allan, what is going on with you? What money, are you owing these boys, talk to me now, said Menna. Allan refused to speak. Okay Allan, when you are ready to talk, you know where you can reach me. What are you doing wearing gang colors, are you in a gang? Its' not a gang, said Allan, they are my family.

Oh I see, said Menna. Allan I want you to come to the youth center tomorrow. The center needs some paintwork done I showed Tess your art work, and Tess is very impressed. Tess has picked out three of your paintings that she wants to purchase for the center. Now how much do you owe these boys, asked Tess, I will pay you forthose three paintings. 300.00 replied Allan. Well, said Tess that is about how much I will pay you for those paintings. Now I want you to report to the center tomorrow, promptly at 3:30, after school. Now do we have a deal? Allans' eyes widened. Tess and Menna saw Allan to his door and ushered him in. See you tomorrow Allan, said Menna if you need a ride give me a call in the morning, before 9am.

Thanks Tess, said Menna. "No problem, girl said Tess". Menna started up the car. Okay Tess the next stop will be Irmas' house.

Tess and Menna reached Irmas' moms' house and rang the bell. Irmas' mom came to the door. (Everyone called Irmas' mom "Mother Thompson" this is what she preferred to be called). When Menna and Tess entered Mother Thompson' home she ushered us up to Irmas' room. Mother Thompson, and the children were baking cookies. Menna and Tess entered Irmas' room, Irma was alert, but she was on some type of medication from her therapist. Irma how are you today, asked Menna? Hey girl what's' been going on with you asked Tess. Irma just started to cry. I can't take this, said Irma., Things just keep coming upTess, do you remember a case at the college about a year ago, where the students were turning up missing? Twelve years ago to be exact, replied Menna. Well, said Irma, those students were all troubled, it seems that they had a morphine addiction. Those peoples remains were recovered behind that building 212, there was a cliff which led to the water. Along the side of the cliff, someone stumbled on a cave, that had been man made by breaking into some rocks.

Inside that cave were bones, Hundreds of human bones. The bones had scrapings on them which showed evidence that the flesh had been removed and the bones were suppose to have been discarded. There was also a built in oven: That was used for cooking things. However, one of Geralds' journals turned up at the site.

REFLECTIONS OF LIFE

I have to know Geralds involvement in this. I have some names and places in one journal that I held back. Before I turn this journal over to the police, I need to know what is going on for myself. Menna will you and Tess help me? Asked Irma. Sure. Replied Tess, it will probably do some good to go on a long drive. Where do you want to start asked Menna? At this address in Petersboro, said Irma. This is the doctor who provided the morphine. I need to clear up some things with him.

When do you want to take the trip, asked Menna and Tess? It is about a forty-five minute drive said Tess. The doctor is expecting me Friday. (David can drive along with us, he will be home then, offered Menna. Is that okay with you Tess asked Irma? Sure replied Tess, it will probably be fun.

Where is Gerald at now, asked Menna? Gerald is in hiding, replied Irma. The police are looking for Gerald. He cannot turn himself in until I can come up with something to clear him, "Who else do you have there, asked Tess? There is a man who calls himself their leader , who I must see. He only awakens when the sun goes down. Is he a vampire or something? Asked Menna. No, said Irma he is suppose to be the one who initiated the cult. The other person who is a butcher, prepared those human remains for consumption. That is so grotesque, said Tess. I know, said Irma, but true. Last but not least, there is one guy who escaped just before he was supposed to be sacrificed. Most of these people live in town. Okay Irma, said Menna, we will be in touch before Friday, until thenknow Geralds' involvement in this I have some names and places. In one journal that I held back, before I turn that journal in to the police, I need to know what is going on, for me, and the childrens' sake. Menna will you and Tess help me? Asked Irma. Sure said Menna, where do you want to start? A this address in Petersboro, said Irma, this is the doctor who provided the morphine. I need to clear up some things with him.

Menna and Tess left mother Thompson's house, still having a hard time believing what they had just heard. Tess, said Menna, I think we should notify the fathers' alliance with this one, I agree, said Tess. Finally the last stop was to see Anna;As Menna and Tess pulled into the luxury apartment lot; we noticed Anna and Jerrod returning from an outing. Anna yelled Tess and Menna as they ran over to Anna as if they hadn't seen her in years. Anna looked our way and hurriedly waved us over. We were all so happy to see one another. We filled Anna in on the details, and Anna was ready to go along; Anna was a reporter, and acting her old self again. Anna flashed a very large diamond in front of Menna and Tess, Anna and Jerrod were going to be married.

Finally it was time to drive Tess home; On arriving to Tess'

Moms' house, Menna and Tess went in. Tess took her mail to her room and started to tear open that big box, who could this be from, said Tess. Tess opened the box, and Menna saw Tess' eyes widen in fear. Tess began screaming, no! no! no! shouted Tess, no more. Tess started backing away from the box. What is this , said Menna? Menna started walking towards the box. That walk was the longest walk that Menna had ever taken. Menna looked into the box and screamed. "Oh my God. There in that box was the head of a woman. Menna and Tess turned and fled from the room, phoning the police.

The police arrived and took a report. The officials were in and out of Tess' mothers' house for almost two weeks; Tess held up well, considering, maybe the therapy and the medication was a success.

Menna arrived home after ten pm. The children and Emma were fast asleep; Menna showered and went to bed, tomorrow was a day of work.

"Nona pull that bib up"; Manna said, Nona, I need to talk to you after class; After class Nona came up to Menna. Nona said Menna, this behavior you are displaying is indecent and not ladylike. It will get you in trouble if you don't be careful. What, asked Nona? Nona your tops are always so small, and your skirts are always to short, young ladies do not dress that way, young lady, you follow the dress code for school. Nona sauntered off, as if she didn't care one way or another. Nona your box called Menna, what is in here anyway? Stuff, replied Nona, as she took the box from Mennas' hand.

Nona had a little ice blue box,that she always carried with her, wherever she went. I guess you would call it he security blanket. Nona was having a hard time with self-respect. Nona was a foster child, this has been Nonas' third foster home in two months.

That day was fill of excitement; The childrens, annual picnic was coming up in two weeks and the preparations were more extreme this year, since the children had come up with a theme for their annual picnic, the children displayed some very good ideas, for games, etc. Menna hurried to her class, Menna smelled smoke in the hallways, cigarette smoke. The smell had to be coming from the girls bathroom. Menna went to investigate, and there was Nona; with a couple of her friends. Girls, what is going on, asked Menna? The girls tried to flush the cigarettes down the commode, but Menna had already seen them. Okay girls, said Menna. I think that after school detention is in order here. I will be, contacting parents, now lets get to class. Everybody hurried off to class, except Nona, for Nona could barely walk. Nona re you intoxicated, asked Menna? Nona muttered something and passed out right in Mennas' arms.

Menna put her arm behind Nonas' neck, and usheres Nona to the nurses office. Menna laid Nona down and phoned for her parents to come and pick her up. Nonas'ents finally arrived to escort Nona home; Don't forget her blue box, said Menna. The day went on as usual. That night Menna tried to figure out ways in which to make Nona recognize her self-worth.. Perhaps Nona and some of the girls can sponsor a fashion show for the parents' night, at 50 cents a ticket, and the money from the plant sale we could purchase more computer software.

That Tuesday, was nuts at Mennas' house. Rachel couldn't find her homework, because Mark had used it to make airplanes with, which just happened to land in the fish tank In turn Rachel hides Marks' shoe. Meanwhile, Menna is in the shower yelling for the dog (Mohamad), to bring back her bathrobe. This says something for the day said Menna. Menna grabbed for her towel and covered herself, putting the dog up, and letting Mark out of the closet, in which Rachel had locked him in. And Rachel, just sitting there and combing her dolls' hair. As if nothing were going on, and I think that I am about to lose it.

Menna held her breath and counted to ten, and proceeded. Now Rachel, give Mark back his shoe; I can't said Rachel. Why not, asked Menna? I threw it out the window, said Rachel. Oh Rachel, you didn't, said Menna, as Menna looked out the window, and spotted Marks' shoe on the roof ledge. Mark, said Menna, I guess you will just have to wear shoes today instead of sneakers. Rachel you will just have to make your homework up tonight. Now kids, said Menna, behave yourselves. Menna hurriedly dressed and out the door her and the children went. On arrival to school that day, Menna discussed the idea with Dr. Woods, concerning the fashion show. Dr. Woods thought that it was a good idea. Now to present the idea to Nona, thought Menna, as she took the stairs up to her class. Menna walked the length of the hall , she happened to look out the window. Menna saw Nona waiting outside for someone. Shouldn't she be in class, Menna said to herself. Menna hurried down the stairs to find out why Nona was not in class. As Menna made it to the door, a car pulled up and Nona started to get inside . Hold it Nona, said Menna, where do you think you are going? Don't you dare get into that car, said Menna. The driver hurriedly pulled away and Nona turned towards Menna. Nona was intoxicated, and Menna could smell the alcohol on her breath. Nonas' face was swollen and puffy. Nona what happened to you, asked Menna? Just then, that car pulled back up alongside the curb, the driver, was telling Nona to get inside.. Menna said, Nona isn't going with you today or any other day. The young man was in his early twenties and Nona was only fourteen. Nona, asked Menna? did he do this to you? Nona did not answer, she just stood there in a daydream. Nona, I think you had better come with me, said Menna.

The man jumped out of the car and grabbed Nona into the car. Nona followed along. Menna pulled Nonas' free arm, and said if you don't leave, I will have you arrested. (That didn't scare him. He became more hostile). Menna carried a whistle around her neck, which she used in case of emergencies. Menna blew the whistle loud, over and over again. Menna knew that the dogs were close; The man jumped into the car and pulled off.

This is starting to get serious Nona, said Menna. I don't know what you call yourself doing, but you had better start thinking about a life for yourself, before its' to late. I recognize that guy, Nona, with all his gold jewelry, he doesn't respect himself, do you really think that he respects you. "Who cares anyway, said Nona as she began to cry. I care said Menna, believe me, I care. Yeah, I know you care, said Nona. Just like my alcoholic mother, you care; Get away from me, said Nona. Nona, said Menna, take my card, call me anytime of the day or night. Nona took the card and ran down the street.

Menna notified the child services and the foster parents of Nona. Menna left a message for the parents to please call Menna at home, if there is any word from Nona. Menna needed an empty room, any room. Menna needed to pray, Menna went inside the faculty room. Dear God, said Menna, you said that you would be sending me Elijah, to help me, God where is he. I need help now, don't let me lose Nona. God, Satan is winning, he cannot win; he cannot have another one, please help. AMEN At that moment Menna felt a hand caress her forehead, Menna did not see anyone., but she felt a presence. Menna said Amen. As Menna got up to leave, she felt a pat on the shoulder blade. At that moment Menna felt hopeful.

Jerrod is a widow with two children and he is trying to pick up the pieces of his life. We are good for each other, said Anna.

That afternoon, there was a message on Mennas' answering machine for her to contact Nona, at her foster parents home; (thank you God, said Menna). That Tuesday night the children were exceptionally quiet. Mark and Rachel didn't do much fussing, I guess they did it all that morning. Okay Mark and Rachel, you children have got homework to do lets' get to it. After the children settled down, Menna returned her phone call.

Hello, Nona, said Menna , are you alright? I don't know replied

Reflections of Life

Nona. I have to talk to someone. (Are your parents at home? Asked, Menna). No replied Nona, they are at work; (Okay Nona, it is 7:30, I can be there by 9:00p.m. would that be alright, asked Menna?) Yes, replied Nona. I will see you at nine said, Menna. Menna hung up the phone. Looking over the childrens' homework, Menna could not help but asked herself; What could be wrong, oh well said Menna, I will soon find out.

By 8:30, Menna had the children in bed and had gotten Mrs. Thomas to sit with the children. That drive to Nonas' house was longer than Menna thought. Menna arrived to Nonas house and rang the doorbell. Nona immediately opened the door. Nona, said Menna you should have asked who it was first. Nona just stood there with a nervous look on her face. Nona said, Mrs. Phillips, I am afraid for my life.. "Why Nona, said Menna, what on earth do you mean? Nona left the room, and returned with her blue box, as Menna sat down on the sofa, Nona opened the blue music box cover. Menna could not believe her eyes. Nona pulled out, eight little blue books, which looked like telephone number books.

Nona handed Menna the books; As Menna opened the first book, and to her surprise, there in that book were names and ages of children, ranging in ages from age five to sixteen, who had dates with older men, some of these patrons were names of well-known and respected people.

Nona, where did you get these books from, asked Menna? I found them, said Nona. I found them in the back seat of a cab I took home yesterday. Does anybody know that you have these books., asked Menna? Not yet replied Nona, but they will; Nona, we have got to turn these books over to a federal agent; But first let us find a safe haven for you. We can give the books to the Fathers' Alliance, and they will make sure that the books reach the right hands. These books will be safe, said Menna.

Menna phoned her uncle, who was a FBI retiree, and in less than twenty minutes, someone was there to take Nona to a safe place. Nonas' whereabouts were confidential. Nonas' family and me were all placed under a protection screen, which lets' everyone know the seriousness of this matter. Officials felt that the children and me needed protection to and from school and work. I don't think that I was afraid, I think that I was more worried about the danger that these young children were in.

We were instructed to wait and see who was interested in these books. The mayors' task force set up a satellite headquarters at Nonas' home> Everything was done so secretly, so expertly, so as not to draw attention to oneself. Mennas' uncle, watched Nonas' home. (He was a FBI retiree, and a member of the fathers' alliance).

Nonas' home was watched via, a van parked across the street, just behind Nonas' home.

Theres' that two-bit hood, pulling up in front of Nonas' house, radio one father, be ready. Joey pulled up into the driveway, got out of the car and rung the bell, a member of the Mayors' Task Force pulled Joey inside of the house. Who sent you, said one of the officials to Joey. I cannot tell you that, said Joey,. They will kill me. (You don't work for them anymore, from now on you work for us, said the official). Now just in case you get any bright ideas, here is your insurance, said the official, as two others, pushed Joeys' brother from behind a curtain, so that Joey could see him.

Joey' brother was blindfolded, and his hands were restrained behind his back. Joeys' brother was a drug addict. Joey loved his brother, and he did not want to see his brother hurt. Okay man, said Joey, what do you want me to do?

There was a plan, and Joey along with three of his close friends' were going to help to pull it off. It took the taskforce exactly one week to mastermind the plan. The apartment complex across the street was built and operated by the city of Buffalo.

The following week, some of the women (who were in the military), moved into the complex; The apartment complex residents had been relocated. The whole building was empty, except for the women, coming and going. Bringing in and taking out needed material in a way that made things look so normal. The phones were busy, busy, busy, that week; The task force used plants to set up dates with these innocent children, in such a way that every child in that book would be at two separate meeting places at the same time. The plan would take a month to complete; But over two hundred children as young as five years old, used for prostitution, was a bitter pill to swallow. The Mayor, was outraged

Joey and his friends were more cooperative and eager to help than everyone had planned. The children came from all walks of life; different races, and different nationalities. I have to say that the nation of Islam also gave their support. Most of the plants came via the nation. The whole city was in an uproar and all good people were included. The nation did donate the second apartment bldg.

The actual plan was to go down at exactly, 10:00pm. That night, everything looked to be in order; The plants were costumed, and sent to their posts.

A PLANT IS A PERSON USED TO INFILTRATE AND CORRECT A WRONGDOER..

About one hour later the children started to arrive; Before anybody knew what was going on, the men had took back every child that was in that book (two children were killed, I am sorry to say).

REFLECTIONS OF LIFE

The pain in those childrens' faces, was something you could not begin to imagine, kidnapped children, and children from all walks of life, children from all over the world. The complex was set up as a home away from home for theses kids.

The building was expanded, just that building took up over a whole block; Sleeping quarters were accomplished for the children, the women of the Islam Nation, took children into one complex. It took the official, exactly three days to make suitable living conditions for the children. Getting these children home, would take some doing. This was going to take some doing if the children had a suitable home environment, would have to be investigated.

After six months of investigations, locating parents, all children were returned home, except for thirteen who were placed in foster care.

This incident did a lot of good. Troubled homes were targeted. Help was available. The city gained notoriety and worldwide donations for a cause. This was the area that only a closel knit community could handle. Donations kept pouring in on a worldwide scale. More jobs were created, due to the caseload. Children were sent here from all over the globe, and the children continue to come. Funding was more available, which did not hurt the economy any.

The city that nobody cared about had proved to be the most riches city in the whole world and the only city that could be trusted to handle such a delicate situation. I guess a little love and goodness, along with a firm belief in God, along with respect for one another and for those things that God gave us is truly a most magic potion for happiness.

REFLECTIONS OF LIFE

Those Reflections' Of Life can be a kind of life; As we live, and as we learn, we find happiness is a gift well earned; As we continue our life, in the Reflections of Life, saddled down to strife; And Troubling times, basically what we need is to love and be loved;
    A priceless gift, given us somewhere from above.

    Those Reflections of Life can lead us to the brink.
    That brink of destruction, because we lack, the missing link.
    Oh, if we all could do it right the first time.
    But those reflections of Life, is a long long, winding road. Full of challenges, and deceptions, that we too choose to hold.

And if by chance we make it back from the tumult
We choose to face:
Please remember those "Reflections of Life".
All the pain, all the grief, the strife;
And hurry back home to your perfect layed –back life.

Love to all my brothers and sisters worldwide

To Be Continued, Be sure to look for Reflections Of Life. A New Generation. A powerful and compelling drama based on the lives of our children going over the edge.
WARNING: Live your life cautiously, but to the fullest; Determine that legacy that we unwittingly pass on.

A NEW GENERATION CONTINUES

Allan had really grown-up to be a fine young man, thought Menna. As Menna, Tess, Collette and Anna watched Allan, and his new bride' posed for wedding picture in front of the wedding cake.

Allan had become an aspiring young artist, who owned his own publishing company. Allans father had left Allan his legacy. After Allan',grandparents, passed away seven years ago. A man and a woman, who had been searching for Allan, found him. Allans' natural father had fathered Allan when he and Allans' natural mother were going to be married. However, Allans father whose name was also Allan Sr. And Allans mother (Alana). Lost touch, when Alana did not fit in. So Allan was brought up not knowing his real father. Allan knew his stepfather. Allans' stepfather and mother, had bonds which they left Allan in the event of his death. Over the years those bonds became priceless. Allan had been blessed, Allan was now a wealthy young man.

Allans' bride was his high school sweetheart. Her name was Cecilia. Cecilia was young, beautiful, and pregnant. Cecilia was twenty- two years old, had a past history of a amphetamine addiction.. Allan was always there for Cecilia, pulling her through a mountain of problems. I guess Allan just felt that it was his responsibility to be there for her.

Cecilia was at one time what seemed to be a very ambitious young lady. Cecilia fought for Allan, she was a girl who had high hopes for her future. Cecilia was at one time on the student council. A cheer leader and had won a scholarship. Cecilia was prom queen. Cecilia had a lot going for her. Cecilia was very bright. At age sixteen Cecilia had accomplished two years of college. After

REFLECTIONS OF LIFE

Cecilias' father was killed in the line of duty ..after the Korean war, when Cecilias' father became a decorated officer. (This is when he was killed in the line of duty.). Cecilia seemed to lose her ambition. Cecilia just one day stopped caring. I guess that is why Allan was so dedicated to her, he knew the real Cecilia. I guess you could say that Allan cared enough for the both of them.

Cecilia asked Allan, which tie do you think goes better with my suit. The dark blue one, replied Cecilia, as she continued to file her nails. I should be taking on some new clients after this night, said Allan.

The art shows brought in a stream of new clients, Allan had done well with his business, now everybody wanted a piece of the action. At one time Allan could not even get so much as a sponsor for his shows.

Cecilia owned two boutiques in the heart of the city. Cecilia was a dance instructor, who also ran a dance studio. Allan and Cecilia are doing really well. They were ,both busy, busy, busy, all the time. Allan hone, said Cecilia, zip me up.

Sure honey said Allan as he zipped up Cecilias' dress. Cecilia went to the bathroom and climbed atop the sink, reaching on the top of the linen closet. Cecilia pulled out a bottle of pills, popping two pills into her mouth, two pep pills, and Cecilia was ready to go.

Cecilia, called Allan, we will be late. Coming dear, said Cil, as she left the bathroom and put her arm into her fur coat , which Allan was holding out for her to put on. Allan and Cecilia hopped into the chauffeur driven limo and was on their way. The art show moved right along, Allan gained three clients in the first hour of the show. Cecilia and Allan were having cocktails with a client, when Cecilia excused herself to go to the ladies room. (Hold it girl you are taking to much, said Cil to herself).

Allan thought about Cecilia and the problem she had with the barbiturates. Allan knew that Cecilia was using far to many diet pills. Allan had tried talking to Cecilia and expressing his concern, but Cil just would not listen. Allan had dealt with this problem before with Cil throughout college. Cecilia always managed to come around before the problem took over her being. Only this time, Allan feared that Cil may, not come around. Allan had to come up with a solution fast.

Well, Allan said Mr Klein, as he sipped his drink. I would like to schedule a meeting with you at my villa, next Thursday at 8:00p.m., to discuss an advertising contract for my work. I am willing to pay top dollar for good work. Do you think that you can keep this meeting, bring the wife along, the more the merrier. Certainly, Mr. Klein, you won't be sorry, that, you chose our company., We aim to please. Wonderful, replied Mr. Klein, d we have a date, yes we sure do replied Allan as he shook Mr. Kleins hand. Afterwards, Allan went to mingle with the rest of the crowd. Two hours later, still no Cecilia, Allan checked the womens bathroom, the lobby and had Cil paged. Allan realized that Cecilia had left.

The woman got off the bus, she always felt nervous coming home from work, just before midnight. It was always so dark and quiet. Looking over her shoulder the woman noticed a strange car off into the shadows. As the woman turned the corner, a man grabbed her from behind. The stranger threw the woman into the side of a building. She tried to scream but no sound would come out. The stranger forced the woman into a deserted building. He brutally beat and raped an innocent woman. The stranger phoned for an ambulance and reported the location where the brutally beaten woman was.

The stranger jumped into his car, which was parked away from the scene, as the stranger started up the car and put in a CD, which played soothing music. He began to take off his gloves. And finally ,his ski mask. It was late, but the stranger need to see his father. The stranger pulled into the parking lot of the sanitarium, and went up the back stairs, to see his father. When Gerald ll arrived to his fathers' room, Irma was there visiting with Gerald Sr. Gerald ll walked over to his mother (Irma), He put his head in his mothers' lap and called out for his father. To talk to him., Gerald Sr. just kept staring into space. Gerald Sr, had no recollection to the world around him.

Hi Ermine, said Rachel (Mennas daughter). How was your date last night? Oh hi Rachel, said Ermine, I guess Terrence is okay, he is not much of a conversationalist. You know. Well said Rachel you can't win them all. Listen Ermine (Irmas daughter age 19), I have tickets to the ballet this Saturday, would you and Terrence like to go? Sure replied Ermine, why don't we take mommas limo for that night, said Ermine. Sounds good to me, said Rachel, pick us up at 8pm. Maybe afterwards we can have dinner or something. See you then said Rachel as she placed the phone into its' cradle. Rachel and Ermine were both attending Yale University. Rachel and Ermine lived off campus in a security building. We were spending our springbreak at home. Momma, Irene wants to know do you need anything from the store? Asked Ermine. Tell Irene to be home in time for dinner. Irene was Irmas twenty-one year old daughter who was almost a pediatrician, unlike her mother who was a pediatrician. Ermine was following the footsteps of a family of doctors.

Gerald 11 was an airplane pilot, age 23, Gerald 11 was married to Angela who was a stewardess. Angela and Gerald 11 owned and operated a travel agency in there spare time. Gerald 11 walked into his plush home and handed his housekeeper his coat and pilots' hat, and grabbed his two boys age 21, up in a big bear hug. Geralds' wife Angela was on a flight. Gerald 11 sat in his study, just staring, not uttering a word. Gerald stood up and walked out of his house and headed for his car to one of the hot spots in town. Gerald 11 cruised the streets looking for his next victim. Gerald watched her walk t the ramp and put her car keys into the lock.

Gerald 11 grabbed the young woman from behind, pulling her into a nearby alley, there Gerald 11, raped and beat his victim. Gerald phoned for help as he always did before leaving his victim. Gerald 11 drove to the country- side, pulling his car into a grassy field, which was land owned by his father. Gerald 11 got out of the car pacing backwards and forwards., fist clenched, hitting at the air, grinding his teeth and mumbling some sort of foreign tongue jibberish. Gerald 11 took his right shoulder, ramming it into the car several times. Gerald 11, backed away from the car several steps backward Gerald 11, with all his strength, ran headfirst into the rear of the car, foaming at the mouth, and finally accomplishing what he tried to accomplish, sleep. Gerald 11 had knocked himself out. Gerald ll lay there for several hours, sleeping away the pain he felt inside. Finally Gerald 11 went into the house and cleaned himself up, before starting home. Gerald ll breathed a sigh of relief, he felt better now.

Charlotte, said Collette. I don't think now is a good time for you to be a hanging around in those streets with a rapist loose. I am eighteen years old, and you don't tell me what to do, said Charlotte. Well, said Collette I forbid you to go out this evening. The car pulled up in front of the house. Collette could hear loud music. Along with loud voices , as Charlotte rushed out the door. Collette looked out and saw about four men, hanging out the car windows. Egging Charlotte on, Charlotte jumped into the front seat and the car sped off.

Charlotte was always going off with those strange men., always gone for days. One time Charlotte left for two weeks.

Collette, had acquired a job, with the Federal Agency, due to her undercover work, Collette had received a promotion, and her own office, Staring out the window Collette prayed that nothing would happen to Charlotte, Collette had the reassurance that if anything happened to Charlotte, it would be harm that Charlotte brought on herself.

Collette passed Charlenes' room (daughter #2) , Collette heard a loud crash, as Collette rushed into Charlenes' room, there she found Charlene passed out on the bed, with a hypodermic needle implanted into her arm.

Brad, the girls father had left home again. It seems that Brad is always leaving when pressures mounted. Collette never complained much, I guess Collette just learned to live with a fate that she believed she had brought on herself.

Little Bradley was now fifteen years old; As Little Bradley and two of his friends, busted out the car windows of a car that they had never seen before, you could hear the sounds of police sirens in the background. Lucas, hot wire the car, ordered Little Bradley, we are going to take off the corner liquor store. Little Bradley, protested Jonas, I don't think this is such a good idea. Who do you think you are talking to, said Little Bradley as he walked over to Jonas, hitting him in the head with a pistol. Jonas fell to the pavement, blood everywhere. Little Bradley began to kick and spit on him. Jonas was unconscious.

Little Bradley and Lucas, picked up Jonas' lifeless body and threw him in the back seat of the stolen car. The car speedily pulled off. Little Bradley pulled into tan alleyway not far from the liquor store. The pair went inside the liquor store.. Bradley and Lucus, the pair demanded cash; The cashier did not argue, he forked over the cash to the pair. The pair locked the cashier in a storeroom, tying his arms and legs, and covering his mouth. Shooting out camera lenses, the two fled on foot, leaving Jonas unconscious in the stolen car.

Jonas woke up from his unconscious state, looking around him. Jonas knew that they would be back for him. Jonas dragged himself from the car, and looked for a safe place to hide himself. Jonas saw a dumpster, Jonas crawled behind the dumpster, amongst a bunch of cardboard boxes, and loss consciousness again. Jonas had nowhere to go anyway, he had run away from the orphanage, usually on really cold nights he would sleep at Little Bradleys' or Lucas house after their parents were asleep. One time he hid out in Lucas attic for a whole winter.

All Jonas knew, was that he did not want to go back to the orphanage. Jonas never knew his parents, but he knew that he had to have parents, or else how could he have gotten here. Maybe one day his parents would come for him, but for now he only knew that Little Bradley, Lucas, and him looked out after one another, and he knew that they would be back for him.

A LEGACY CONTINUES

Menna set up a meeting with her four children., the children were older now. Menna wanted her children to familiarize, themselves, with her and Davids' memoirs. Menna felt that her children needed to know certain details about the past. Things that would help them to understand how these children that they grew up with, might someday need their help.

Menna felt as if she was passing on a legacy of ill fortune to her children, but deep down Menna knew that if any life is worthy to be a part of the earth, that is a life worth saving. Rachel was the first to arrive. Rachel was a school- teacher at the Community School. , Rachel had met and fell in love with Bret. Bret was a military man just like her father. He had graduated college via the military, and was now a military policeman. A war brat,, following in his fathers' footsteps. His father was a colonel, and Brets' mother was an army nurse.

Rachel and Bret planned to be married one day. Rachel felt that she needed to make a self, sufficient life for herself, so no date was set. Bret graduated college two years after Rachel arrived to school.

Hi mom, said Rachel as she entered the door. Hi Rachel, said Menna, as Menna brushed Rachels' cheek. Momma asked Rachel, what is this about? Well dear, said Menna, we will wait for your brothers to arrive, before I disclose my reasons. Dear could you help me with these, said Menna as she handed Rachel an, hordouerve tray. Sure momma, where is dad? He had a meeting with the elder chapter of the Fathers' Alliance. Mark, Chad and Matthew have joined with your father that is one of the reasons for this meeting.

Finally, Matthew and Chad arrived. The boys were professional athletes. Matthew played college football and was constantly on the go. Matthew chose to live at home and attend school. Matthew was dating Helena. Helena was attending the local college. And was a professional dancer. Helena moved here five years ago with her parents. Hal and Helen, who owned and operated a family inn.....

Matthew had met Helena at college. A well –known, college. Chad played basketball and wanted to be a coach. Chad put a majority of his time into working with wayward children. Chad wasn't serious, about anyone as of yet, however, he dated the firls from the church we attended. I often noticed how Chad and Father Hillards' daughter often exchanged glances during services. Selena (ministers' daughter), wanted to be a doctor. Chad was studying law, but he also enjoyed being a big brother.

Hi mom, said the two boys as they grabbed a handful of finger sandwiches. Hunting down the milk. The two boys startes a milk tug of war. Boys, said Menna, ho horse playing, and watch my breakables, cautioned Menna. They are so immature, said Rachel, as she gave the boys that evil eye. Rachel, you are just mad because Tyrone dumped you, said Chad. He didn't dump me, I dumped him, and I thank you to mind your business, said Rachel. The boys started to tease Rachel, grabbing her telephone number book and throwing it backwards, and forwards from Matthew to Chad. Boys, said Menna, stop teasing your sister. The boys sat on the chaise, acting as if the previous incident had not occurred.. Rachel, still fussing, gave the two a pinch as she went out on the deck, reaching for an apple. Ouch, said Matthew and Chad as they studied the sports page.

Finally Mark and David arrived. How did the meeting go, asked Menna? Looking good, said David as he tenderly kissed Menna. Hey sis, said Mark. The two goons have been causing problems? Not us replied Matthew and Chad as they faced downward at the sports pages. (The two boys respected Mark, their elder brother, and they listened to him, oftentime going to Mark for advice). Where is Emma, asked Mark? Emmas' at her embroidery class, said Menna.

Well, said David as he hit a glass crystal with his spoon lightly. I think that it is time to get to the business at hand. The meeting will come to order. The rest of the family exited to the deck of the house, and seated themselves on the chaise. Menna went and bought out three journals from the safe. Menna had planned to publish her journals.

Okay children, said Menna, these journals are the history of our friends and family, which dates back over fifteen years. We will divide the three journals up into six, and children please follow along, you are old enough to understand. Menna began the story, Menna covered the time dating back to when she was a little girl and first came to this city, Menna went on to familiarize the children with her friends and the offspring of her friends, the story went on for over two hours.

The children had tons of questions. Finally David, said, children, we are having this meeting so that you will understand some of the problems that your friends have endured for past and present. This is one of the main reasons for the Fathers' Alliance. We cannot just turn our backs on those whom we have loved, or brothers and sisters need us. In the past the results have produced some very respected and influential people;.

This group of people, have strengthened our legacy. And it just keeps getting better.

Children all that we ask, is that you take the time and give of yourself. Take the time to recognize your brothers and sisters and help them if needed. With the right caring attitude our legacy will be a strong one, through the lives of our brothers. Are there any questions, asked Menna? Just one, said Rachel, Mark will speak for all of us.

We need a twenty-four hour workable number, for the Fathers' Alliance. Yes, said David, that number has been activated. Here is a copy of all the information that you will need, and should know. People affiliated with the alliance as well as agencies we confer with.

So ends the meeting. The children stayed for dinner, and we enjoyed the remainder of the evening together.

That night, Menna was restless. Sleep would not come. Menna had not touched bases with her friends. With David being home on a full time basis, now, Menna did not have the spare time she once had. Menna knew that something wasn't right, her spirit self told her that things were chaotic. The peaceful calm was gone. Afraid to check into saddened situations, Menna tried to sleep. Menna tossed and turned. Menna was itching all over, as if she had a rash or something. What was that, said Menna as she noticed a very large shadow look as if it leaped from her body, just as quickly as Menna saw the thing, it was gone. Menna said, my eyes are playing tricks on me again. Menna dismissed this from her mind.

Menna looked at her clock, it was 3:47am. Menna finally drifted off to sleep, or was Menna sleep? Menna saw that shadow being, within sight of her peripheral vision (peripheral vision; ability to see out of the corner of your eye). However, the crature seemed so close till Menna felt as if she could touch it, Menna was not afraid, it was not fear she felt, but concern, as to what the creature wanted.

The creature reminded Menna of a giant bat, it had wings and eyes, and ears like a bat. The creature had no distinctive features, because it was like a silhouette, and it flew. It was able to make itself invisible, but even so Menna still knew and felt its' presence, and its' warmth. Menna felt wide, awake. Menna tried to talk but the words would not come to the surface, Menna wanted to yell out, "wait a minute, I am still awake, and very much aware". Menna tried to move, but it seemed that her body was built into the bed, she could not free herself from the spot she was in, Mennas' body felt light, weightless. Mennas' breathing became more rapid and faster. The presence of this being so close to her made Menna feel as if strength and energy was leaving her body. Menna felt weak and lifeless.

Menna felt a dead weight lay on her, Menna felt as if she were suffocating. Menna noticed a hollow figure rise from her body, Menna had no reflexes, she could not move, it was as if her body was there in bed, but Menna wasn't

Menna began to see things that am morning, Menna saw children different shapes and different sized, teenagers, young adults, so many different people, in what looked to be a whirlpool with a high wind, which produced a suction or a vacuum force. Menna saw a sign, which read (The Lost Souls) Menna could see the hands and faces. The faces were not definitive. Their eyes were wide opened. They did not blink. The souls had their hands reaching upwards as if they were reaching for the heavens, trying to tear away from the vacuum.

There was a figure, which looked hideous and evil, looking down at the lost souls, with a wide grin on its' face. Not offering any help, the thing was increasing the suction power.

There was a thought coming from this evil mind that Menna could see. There was three sets of bars, behind one set was the men, behind another set of bars, were the women, and behind a third set of bars were the children. The bars were the division, and the men were trying to escape the bars, while the women and children were calling out to them, Menna fought with sounds that were coming from her throat, calling out from behind her throat as loud as she could.

Finally Menna felt a weight being lifted from her body. Menna was able to move her arms and then her legs, ever so slowly, trying not to upset anything. Menna saw a hollow image come from nowhere but slowly drift into her body. Menna began to feel her normal self again.

Menna jumped from her bed at 5:30am, sweat pouring off of her, Menna let out a deep throated scream. Menna sat on the edge of the bed and asked herself, what just happened? Menna was quite shaken up. Menna realized that the occurrence was not just a dream,. Menna saw that large creature slowly fly out of the closed window of her room. Menna headed for the shower.

Menna knew that trouble was closing in. Menna felt that in order for her to be at peace with herself, she knew that she had to take Satan challenges. You know, a lot of people ask themselves. If God does exist, why does he let Satan impose his evil on people, why don't he just do away with him?

Think about it; God must place a lot of trust in us; Satan told God that he could be greater than Him That he could win more souls than God. That he could control all of his people (GODS' PEOPLE). Satan felt the more followers, the more power. Satan is vain, he does not hide what he do, he makes himself known, he loves the attention.

God accepted Satans' challenge, because he had to prove to us that Satan was a liar and a slanderer. God gave Satan a 2000 year reign. Satan was let out of the abyss, and God said "woe to the earth, for Satan is being let loose on you with all the strength and power that he can muster. For he only has a short time. The funny thing is, that inspite, of all this, people still choose to follow Satan, the wages of sin are death.

I guess that is why God is so forgiving. He knows the tricks that Satan pulls on us, and He knows that we are imperfect

Moses was a murderer. Moses killed a man and was a fugitive from the law, on the run. God forgave Moses, Moses is the man that went up into the mountains, and God gave Moses the Ten Commandments, to pass down to the people. Moses went to God, and God took Moses under his wing But it doesn't just stop there. It began somewhere in the Heavens, sometime, long ago before Jesus walked the earth, there were angels in the heavens . One day the angels (a group of angels), got together and decided to overthrow God, by trying to rule the heavens. In the meantime, these very same bad angels were coming down to the earth, taking human form, and having sex with the men and women on the earth. God asked the leader, Jacob, on one occasion, where have you been? Roving about on the earth, said Jacob. Jacob was a troublemaker, the people on the earth was tired of him and his demons coming down to earth and causing problems amongst them, so they chased Jacob up into the mountains. From there Jacob went back to the Heavens. God knew what Jacob had been doing.

However, the angels, who had sex with the women of the earth, produced offspring. (impregnating, the women). Their offspring were giants who roamed the earth terrorizing and bullying the people. They were bad angels descendants. The offspring were called Nephilim God became very angry. God destroyed these Nephilim. The giant, were no more. Jesus said woe to the earth, when he took those bad angels and hurled them out of the heavens to the earth. The earth has been in chaos ever since. The angels The angels had produced a hybrid offspring, flawless in appearance, angelic looking in appearance. The sins of the flesh is big business with Satan. We are given a God given radar. A spiritual self that lets' us know the wolf in sheeps clothes. We make our fate, and we are not prevented from determining our legacy our destiny, it is our choice. Death is the wages for sin of the flesh..

An old wise men once had that problem .His name was David. David had that problem; impure thoughts and actions, however, he paid attention to himself. His spirit self, and asked God for help. When God saw that he was sincere, God took over his spirit self. Satan could not win with that arrangement. God warned Satan don't you dare touch my anointed ones, in spite of all of

Satans' accomplishments, David would have been the ultimate . You see Jesus came from Davids' line. Satan knew that once God took over that spirit self, he knew that once God took over he should listen. So Satan fled.

God is forgiving, because he knows what Satan puts us through. So, you see God is alive and well.

RACHEL'S CALLING

Rachel went into the kitchen, plopping herself down at the kitchen table. Rachel thumbed through the morning newspaper. Emma poured Rachel a cup of coffee; Rachel would you like some eggs, asked Emma? No thank you Emma, said Rachel, I have to hurry or I will be late. (Rachel had a teachers, conference that morning).

Rachel ran for the shower, kissing Menna on the way, and gently rubbing her fathers' head. Rachel showered. As Rachel got out of the shower, she felt something touch her head, and a warm breath close to her face. Rachel became dizzy, but she could not fall. It was like her feet had weights on them, gluing her to the spot that she was in. Rachel felt her breathing quicken. Rachel grabbed hold of the edge of the sink and held on, waiting for that feeling to pass. Rachel sat, on a foot- stool, Rachel had no medical problems. There was a silhouette of a snakelike object, the creature Rachel saw looked like a long black ribbon, its top touched the ceiling of the room, and its bottom touched the floor. This was preventing Rachel from falling. It felt warm, like there was life inside it. It kept appearing and fading away. Rachel could not move from that spot, she was frozen there.

While sitting in the kitchen, sipping her coffee, Menna caught of glimpse of this large silhouetted creature in her hallway leading to the bathroom, The creature was motioning to her to come that way, Menna heard two words "Check Rachel". Menna ran in the direction of the voice, the creature just remained in mid air watching her, Menna, heard the words coming out of the air agin "Check Rachel. Menna neared the bathroom and opened the door. Menna beheld Rachel seated and clutching the sink.

Menna, pryed Rachels fingers away from the sink, and felt Rachels' head.

Dear God, Rachel, you are burning up. Menna pulled Rachel up by the waist, pulling her to her bed. Rachel was breathing, but she was burning up with fever, and fast asleep. Menna removed Rachels robe and put her on a pair of baby doll pajamas Rachel never woke up.

Menna put Rachel to bed and covered her body. The large bat

looking creature was witnessing the whole thing, it just looked on as if it were the right thing to do. Menna just continued taking care of Rachel, the being was not frightening to Menna, somehow Menna felt as if it had been there for a very long time, watching everything. Menna kissed Rachel on the forehead, outened the lights and went back to finish her cup of coffee.

Rachel slept for three days. Menna was familiar with this action that had taken place. Menna began to pray as she sipped on her coffee.

JERRODS SECRET

Jerrod, said Anna, where is it you go every weekend? Nowhere dear, said Jerrod as he kissed Annas' forehead. You know Anna, it has almost been a year since we have heard from Tasha, do you think we will ever see her again., asked Jerrod. I am sure we will said Anna. These letters we have been receiving from Tasha, says that she is alright.k But how can we be sure, that the letters are from Tasha, there is no way of tracing the letters, said Jerrod.

We just have to have faith, said Anna, faith that Taska is safe. The kidnapping plot was foiled via the delivery of the money. The kidnapper is in custody. But the wherabouts of Taska is still unknown. No phone calls, said Jerrod, I need to hear her voice.

Taska was Jerrods daughter by his first marriage'. Taska was nineteen years old, and as far as we knew, she was away at college. Taska had attended finishing school.k Tasha was a pony tail and bobby soxer. Taska chose to wear below the knee skirts and sweaters, with bobby sox, while most of Taskas' friends dressed a little more conservatively. Taska chose to dress more loosely as she called it. Taska was always looking for ways to be different, than what was expected of her. I guess you could say that Taska still had some growing up to do.

Hat Friday, Jerrod packed to leave for his weekend. Anna said, Jerrod we have to talk, I don't like the idea of your going off every weekend without a word. Are you having an affair, asked Anna? Anna, said Jerrod, I love you, I am not having an affair, when the time is right I will disclose to you what this is about, but for now please trust me. Anna stood there looking at Jerrod as he prepared to leave, I will be calling you Anna, said Jerrod, as he intimately kissed Anna and left.

Anna dressed for her lunch date with Menna.; Anna, Menna and Collette had a standing lunchdate for the past three years. However Collette, would not be there. Something was always coming up with Collette. Maybe, Menna and me would go by there after lunch, something had to be wrong.

Anna phoned for the chauffer and she was on her way to pick up Menna. Menna was ready to go, as the limo driver closed the car door, Menna brought up Collettes and Irma. Have you talked to Collette and Irma recently asked Menna? You know, I was thinking about Collette today, we had better go and check after lunch. I agree, said Anna. Menna and Anna, went to a new French restaurant opening, the food was superb. Anna and Menna enjoyed a leisurely lunch. You know Menna, said Anna, I am going to follow Jerrod and find out where he goes every weekend, why don't you come with me?

When do you plan this escapade? Asked Menna. Next weekend, replied Anna. I know that wherever Jerrod goes it is driving distance, we could get Chauncey to drive, he used to be a race car driver at one time.. Anna how do you know that Jerrod drives, said Menna? He could park and take another route. Well, we will soon find out this Friday, said Anna. Anna and Menna paid the check and started on their way to see Collette.

Anna, said Menna have you been checking Katherine? "I see her on a weekly basis, Katy is still in treatment, she hasn't talked since that incident. It is just tearing Katherines' heart' heart up. It has been over seven years now. Little Bradley, just comes and goes whenever he gets ready, Katherine is afraid that he will become a statistic. Why don't we let Matthew work with Little Bradley, said Menna. As I remember, Bradley has the potential for sports, Bradley loved sports.

Why Menna, said Anna. That is a wonderful idea. How are things going with Tess and Terry, asked Anna? I believe that Terrys' healing process is completed. Terry has left school and is now living at home with Tess; It is like Terry doesn't want to leave home. She is sticking close to Tess. Terry did get her Masters Degree at a college near home. Terry is a teacher now. Tess has opened the shelters back up, and Terry donates her time to teach the women and the children, self defense. Terry and Hassan has opened up a school which teaches Tai Kwon Do. It is good to hear that they are doing well, said Anna. Anna said Menna, you could never guess in a million years who Tess is dating, and it looks serious. What, said Anna, who is Tess dating? Joey, Anna; who had a little girl named Theresa? Well Joey found out that Joseph who investigated Tess, back when she was having problems, was his dad. Remember, Joseph, well now he has gotten a couple of promotions. Anyway, he and Tess are in love.

What, said Anna, you mean to tell, me after all these years, Joseph is Joeys' father? And to top that off, Tess and Joseph are in love. Leave it to Menna to bring the good news. I am so happy for everybody. I don't know Anna,, said Menna, something is in the air. I think Satan is loose on us again, I am having those dreams, said Menna. Menna please don't dream said Anna. Once again I just know that something is wrong Anna, I just cannot seem to get away from that feeling, said Menna. Well, said Anna, I guess I will just have to deal with it.

By the way Anna, said Menna, we have to check Dionna and Mrs. Krenshaw; Dionna is still having nightmares, the baby is doing fine now, but it is to early to tell what that traumatizing experience did to her, we are going to have to keep an eye on those two. That type of experience if not handled properly will come back to haunt you. The only safeguard from that type of thing, is plenty of spiritual food.

Amen, girl, said Anna: Menna, said Anna, I am glad we are friends. That goes without saying, Anna. I love you too girl, said Menna. Okay, enough of that mushy stuff, said Anna. Gosh Anna, said Menna, so many lives, so much work to be done.

The drive to Collettes' house seemed so long. Anna and Menna knew that something was wrong, well we would soon be there, and then we would know first hand.

Anna could not help but feel an ,uneasiness, about Jerrods' comings and goings. Anna had to know what was going on with the man she had chose to spend the rest of his life with. Anna trusted Jerrod, that, was the most important thing. For love and trust would pull us through. But what if Jerrods' secret is to, much for me to bear God, asked Anna to herself "Pay attention to yourself, Anna, and follow. Let me be your guidance and direction, and rest-assured, that everything will be alright. Anna looked around at Menna. Menna did you say something, asked Anna? I heard a voice that spoke to me. (Were you praying Anna, asked Menna? Yes, replied Anna, that is your spirit self talking. Pay attention and follow, said Menna.).

Terry would you answer the door, said Tess, as she towel dried her hair; Momma, it is a package for you, Terry said, as she signed her name. I wonder what could it be, said Terry as she yelled for her hair. Momma, it is a package for you, Terry said as she signed her name. I wonder what could it be, said Terry as she yelled for her mom, and started to tear open the package.

Tess yelled, no Terry., as she ran into the family room where Terry was, dripping water everywhere. Terry don't open that package. Tess picked up the phone and dialed Josephs' number.

Tess thought back to the time when Terry had been abducted; Joseph had guided Tess through some really difficult times in her life. Tess owed her life to Joseph, both past and present.

One day while at the shelter, taking inventory. Tess noticed a car parked in front of the shelter. Tess had seen that car before, and she just about knew who was in it. Tess slowly walked over to the car, and asked Koseph is there anything that she could get for him? A sandwich, coffee Joseph looked up at Tess, and Tess looked into his eyes. There was a closeness there, that Tess never knew was there, it was almost as if God had chosen Joseph for Tess and was letting Tess know how she felt.

Joseph and Tess started dating, and the sparks began to fly, Tess and Joseph were in love and had been in love for years. Hi Joe, said Tess, another package has arrived. "Don't do anything Tess, you and Terry leave the house until I get there."

Tess quickly hung up the phone; "C'mon Terry said Tess, lets' go outdoors, I will explain later. Terry obeyed her mother.

Fifteen minutes later, Joseph arrived with a bomb squad. The men went inside the house. Joseph rushed over to Tess to comfort her; Tess felt safe in Josephs' arms. The contents of the package consisted of a teddy bear that Terry had owned when she was a little girl, only it couldn't be Terrys' teddy bear, Terrys' bear is stored away in the attic, how could the stranger had gotten in to the attic, said Tess?

Joseph went to the attic to check the contents. Joseph asked Tess to come up. Tess climbed the stairs, and to her surprise, the things were there, the bear, must have been a look a like. Tess and Joseph too the teddy bear downstairs to compare it with the bear that had come in the mail. The details were identical. Even down to the missing button on the vest. Tess, said Joseph, I think it is time that you have that talk with Terry. Yes, I think so, said Tess. I will see you tonight about seven, said Joseph as he held Tess close. Joseph turned to leave. Tess and Terry retreated to the family room. It was time Terry knew the truth.

Joseph was a tall man, who walked with a quiet calm about himself, as if he was always trying to solve something. Joseph had a nervous habit of always using his thumb to scratch the underside of his chin. Joseph and his son Joey had become very close throughout the years. Joseph knew that he had to find this serial killer, he knew that he would not give up until this person was caught. Joseph felt that it was a possibility that this person or persons were trying to get to Tess and Terry. Joseph believed that this person was somewhere close. Joseph decided to put his time and energy into nailing this person. His identity was known, now to go after him, thought Joseph.

Joseph went to his last known address, the man had packed and left the boarding house. This is going to be more difficult than I thought, said Joseph. But I plan to nail this creep, said Joseph to himself.

REFLECTIONS OF LIFE

The stranger walked into the hospital waiting room and registered. Mr. Cahill the nurse called out, please come with me. The stranger followed the nurse to a private room. The stranger removed his street clothes, and got into a hospital gown, and waited to be examined by the doctor.

The doctor came in and examined the stranger. The surgery was scheduled for tomorrow morning, said the doctor to the patient. That morning the stranger waited in silence. The anesthetic was now taking effect. The stranger was taken to the operating room. He saw figures, but due to the anesthetic, everything was a blur. The stranger vaguely saw a team of surgeons working on him. Everything was in bits and pieces, a blur.

What seemed like minutes, was really hours. The stranger woke up, covered in bandages. The doctor and nurse walked in and began to remove the bandages from the strangers face. The nurse handed the stranger a mirror, he had a whole new identity, no one would recognize him now, the plastic surgery had went well.

The doctor looked on in awe, while under the anesthetic the stranger had said some really horrid things. Could the things that the stranger mumbled, while under sedation be true? Could this man be a killer as he had pronounced himself to be?

The doctor had recalled many years ago, while he was still in medical school, a case in which several women had been murdered, via the battered womans' shelter. The doctor knew Tess Harper, since the doctor on staff at the Saint Josephs' hospital, tended to the women at the shelter. The doctor felt that it was his civil duty to report what he had just heard. The stranger mumbled names of the dead women, the doctor knew who these women were. His daughter had been a victim. The stranger said that this time next week, Tess and Terry would be dead. Who was that federal agent, his name was Joseph something, he had been to the hospital several times with tons of questions. I should have a card of his somewhere around here, said the doctor.

Menna readied herself for the concert that Friday night. Menna had planned everything so perfectly, and completely, until the car gave them trouble, now Menna had not planned for that.

Those boys are murder on a car, said David as he rushed in throwing off his shoes to shower and change. Is the car working, asked Menna, as she put her earrings on. Yes dear, said David, a little brake fluid goes a long way. "How much time do we have, we should make it dear, said Menna. We still have about an hour before curtain time, we will just have to have dinner after the show, said Menna.

Wow! You two look great, said Rachel, as she took twenty dollars from Mennas' wallet. "Thanks sweetheart, said David, not so bad for the ice age, ha dear, said David as he tugged on the bottom of his dinner jacket. Have a good time, mom and dad, said Rachel, as she turned her attention to her telephone conversation. David and Menna quietly walked out the door.

Gosh Bret, said Rachel, I cannot make it tonight, I have tons of work to complete; Just remember the ballet Saturday night. "I guess I will just have to compose myself till then, said Bret. Bret I have to go now, said Rachel, I will talk to you later.

Rachel put the phone back into its' cradle and turned to her stacks of childrens homework. At that moment the telephone rang again, so loud that Rachel jumped. Hello, said Rachel, somewhat startled. "Hello, said a voice, Rachel is that you, please help me". Cecilia, said Rachel, Cil is that you, said Rachel? Yes this is Cecilia, please come; Cecilia, where are you, asked Rachel? "I do not know, I am at a phone booth on a corner somewhere". Cil, said Rachel, look around for a street sign. "I am at the corner of a street called W. 57th street". What on earth are you doing in that area, asked Rachel? Hold on Cil, I will be right there. Do not go anywhere and give me twenty minutes.

Rachel reached for her car keys and was out the door. My God Cil, My God Cil, hold on, I'll be there, said Rachel as she nervously put the key into the car lock of her van. Rachel seemed to run into more stop lights that night; Cil was Rachels nickname for Cecilia. Rachel honked her horn, as she drove around a stalled car. Rachel, looked at the street signs. Rachel turned down W 57th street. This street is blocks long. Rachel drove on looking for a phone booth where Cil might have, called from, when a van ran into her right headlight.

Rachel parked and waited for the driver to come her way. The driver jumped out of the van waving his hands up in the air, the man was talking so fast that he was speaking Spanish. (Looks harmless enough, Rachel said to herself). Rachel exchanged insurance agents and information, and gave the driver her private number. Mr. Hernandez gave Rachel his private number. The damage wasn't so bad, so the two decided not to use their insurance companies. Each party would be billed for damages. Mr Hernandez, said that he would pay the damages since the accident was his fault.

As Rachel, continued driving, looking for some sign of Cecilia, Rachel noticed a woman slumped down in the doorway of an abandoned building. Rachel pulled out her flashlight and turned it in the direction of the stranger. Oh God, Cil, said Rachel , as she turned her truck around and parked. Rachel ran over to Cecilia. Cil, said Rachel, what on earth has happened to you? Cecilia was all broken up, her face was swollen, and her eyes were swollen shut. Rachel reached for Cecilia. Cecilia started to scream and hit at Rachel. Cecilia it is me, said Rachel. Hold on, while I phone for an ambulance. Cecilia had been beaten beyond recognition. What on earth was Cecilia doing out here? In this area of town anyway, where is Allan? Rachel asked herself.

Rachel phoned Allan to meet her at the hospital. Cecilia has been hurt, Rachel said to Allan. "I knew this would happen, said Allan. Is Cecilia alright,? said Allan. I won't know until the ambulance arrives. Rachel was trying to cover Cecilia with a blanket from her truck.

The paramedics rushed over. Cecilia had a fractured mandible(broken jaw), along with some very bad lacerations to her face. Cecilias beautiful face had been turned into a hideous mask. Who could have done this to Cecilia and why? Said Rachel.

Rachel watched the paramedics work on Cecilia, as tears began to stream from Rachels' eyes. Cil, said Rachel through a cascade of tears. Why did you run away from us? Where have you been? Where did you go Cil, yelled Rachel? Rachel began to cry uncontrollably. Why did you let this happen to yourself? Answer me Cil. Answer me right now, said Rachel. Two of the paramedics rushed over to Rachel, saying, relax. Ms. Phillips, she cannot hear you. Are you a relative?

Rachel handed the medics her identification. Rachel couldn't talk, her body felt numb. The medics knew Menna and Rachel through past experiences. Rachel saw the medics lift Cil onto the stretcher towards the ambulance. Rachel climbed into her truck and put her head face down on the steering wheel, and, asked God for help. Dear God, said Rachel, I need your help. I don't know what happened, all I know is that Cil is with child, my Father, won't you please help her.   AMEN

Irma felt a nagging feeling tugging at her chest. Something just wasn't right. Gerald Sr. was home from the sanitarium. Although, he couldn't talk, due to loss of his tongue. He could use sign language, which he had learned many years ago.

Gerald Sr. could walk, but since his release from the hospital he had been in a wheelchair. That experience has caused Gerald Sr. his mental health. It is as if, someone is trying to prevent me from finding out the truth from Gerald Sr.

Gerald was on medication, and I guess that he would be on medication for a very long while. At this point Irma felt so alone. Gerald Sr. wasn't well, and the children had been affected through exposure to years and years of mental problems. Irma, had to believe that things would be alright.

Gerald 11 sat in the study. The twins were ten months old.

Erik and Gerald lll. The boys were bright and happy babies. Angela was home for the week. Angela loved to create art; Angelas studio was full of her creations. Angela carefully moved the unhardened figures over to a corner of the room, via a push- cart with wheels.

Angela (Gerald11 wife). Went to take a shower, it was time for Angela to have dinner with the twins. After showering, Angela stopped and knocked on Gerald 11 door of his study. No one answered. Angela opened the door and saw Gerald 11 sitting at the desk, with his back facing the door talking to himself. There were strange sounds coming from Gerald 11' throat, almost as if there was another person in the room with him, a deep, throaty, gruesome sound. Gerald 11, said Angela, who are you talking to? I came to call you for dinner. Your favorite sweetheart, pot roast, and mashed potatoes. Gerald 11 swiveled his desk chair in Angelas' direction. Leave me alone, snarled Gerald 11. That voice frightened Angela, I said leave me alone, said Gerald ll again in a loud and forceful tone. Sweetheart, asked Angela? What is troubling you? Gerald 11 stood up, pushed past Angela, and went out the front door. Gerald, Gerald, yelled Angela. Gerald 11 jumped into his Mercedes Benz and drove off, with Angela running behind the car calling out to him. (Gerald 11)

Gerald pulled into a service station: Gerald had to go to the mens' room. Gerald carried with him a silver gray velour bag. As Gerald 11 entered the mens room, he locked the door. Gerald 11 opened the bag, pulling out a ski cap, black leather gloves, tape and a hunting knife. Gerald 11 taped the hunting knife to his abdominal area, sticking mask inside his jacket pocket. Gerald 11 put his gloves on.

Gerald ll got back into his car and headed for a popular night spot. Gerald 11 parked in the alley, facing the club. Gerald ll waited for the sun to go down.

It was 8:00p.m. Gerald 11 sat there for three hours, staring and talking to himself. It seemed as if Gerald 11 was performing some ritual before he went on his hunt. Two different voices escaped Gerald11 mouth. One voice was not even recognizable. Telling Gerald 11 to do things, evil things. The other voice was a high-pitched, cry, a childs cry. I guess you could say crying out in protest. Gerald11 fell asleep, his head on the steering wheel.

Gerald ll woke up at 12:15 midnight. Gerald ll had been asleep over two hours. Gerald11 watched the club.

The young woman left the club, she had argued with her date and was leaving early to go home. She would travel by taxi. The woman had trouble walking., She was intoxicated. Not drunk, just a little unsteady.

REFLECTIONS OF LIFE

A cab raced by, the young woman yelled out for the taxi. The driver kept going. As the woman decided to take the bus, while waiting at the bus stop, Gerald ll turned into the alley. He got out of the car. Gerald ll quietly walked up behind the young woman, grabbing her around the neck with his right arm and holding her mouth with his left hand, he dragged her into the alley. (Gerald ll knew just about every alley in the city. The woman fought, she broke loose from Gerald ll, only to be subdued again. Gerald ll punched his victim, knocking her to the ground. The woman screamed and clawed at Gerald ll. Gerald ll pulled out his hunting knife, that screaming, shut up, shut up, yelled Gerald ll. Gerald ll slashed the womans, throat. After she was dead, Gerald ll raped her. This time Gerald ll killed someone. Gerald ll realized the woman was dead and he ran from the scene.

Getting into his car and frantically driving off, Gerald ll realized that now he was a murderer and a rapist..

Angela, paced the floor of her bedroom. Angela picked up her phone and called mark. Hello, answered Mark, sleepily, who is this? This is Angela, I am sorry to bother you cried Angela. It is Geraldll, he frightens me, he sits and stares all day. He just mumbles things I do not know how to help him. Gerald ll goes off for hours at a time, without so much as a phone call. I am at my wits end, said Angela. Angela calm down, said Mark, I have a shocking story to tell you, maybe it will help you to understand Gerald ll, and why he is so confused.

Mark told Angela of the childrens exposure to the mental illness., and about the cult that he had read about in his mothers' memoirs. Mark told Angela about Gerald Sr. disappearance. Angela just sat there listening. I don't know, said Mark, but maybe this will help you to understand a little about what Gerald11 is going through. You must contact the doctor. The doctor knows the history. His name is Dr L. Lipkowitz, he is the administrator of the sanitarium. I know that he can help you to understand. And I will be right there. Mark hung up the phone .

Mark was Mennas' first-born, her eldest son. Mark had done well for himself, as an inventor. Mark had turned the attic into a studio apartment. He said that his head worked better in that atmosphere. The attic was as big as the whole first floor of the house. Mark was a college graduate and was constantly out of town on business trips. Attending business meetings and a host of other functions. Marks' inventions had made him a millionaire. Mark had some problems in his life (past). A failed marriage, with the end result being Mark had lost everything that he had obtained during the marriage, throughout the years. Mark was that son that Menna worried the most about. Mark was Mennas' firstborn, whom she loved with all her heart.

Menna had always tried to be there for Mark. Mark was the son who was always there when Menna needed him, because he was the oldest. Menna would stay up nights worrying about Mark and his unhappiness, and praying hard that things would work out for Mark.

Mark was a homebody. He loved just staying home, and trying out new ideas that he had in his head. Mark was the firstborn the one that mothers always have to fight the hardest for. The one that you don't let the evil things of the world consume him. The one that you shield from the system.

Mark was always there when Menna needed him. Menna would stay up nights worrying about Marks' happiness, and praying that things would work out for him.

Mark was an inventor, ever since Menna could remember, Mark was always concocting something. Some people just don't understand the strength that comes from a mothers' love. Satan understands well enough. That is why he put so many obstacles in our way, he uses sex as his tool, the only powerful tool that he has.

I watched my first born be destroyed, and knocked down to nothing, and did that ever hurt. Menna saw and felt the pain and sorrow that Mark had carried with him. After years of pain, my firstborn finally healed. With the love and encouragement that only a mothers' love can give. Menna invested in her first borns efforts, his inventions. Menna believed in her son. Mennas' son gave Menna wealth and dedication. All of you mothers, please keep a clear head, and a clean body, for the sake of your child. Mothers' dedicate your lives to your children. AND LADIES THAT IS THE BEAUTY OF LOVE, A MOTHERS' LOVE.

FIRST BORN

Your firstborn is the one who carries those special spices;
In which you took special care to mix, just the right amount
To make him come out just right, trying to accomplish the
Inevitable, which seems so far from sight.
Taking extra special care to not make a mistake
A very tedious Task you do for his namesake.

That firstborn is the one you expect so much from
You expect Him to be perfect, and let Gods' Will Be Done;
You ask God to Guide you and see you through this task;
And he will let you know, how long the pain will last.

REFLECTIONS OF LIFE

The firstborn is the one, in which you wait for that dream to come;
As you lay sleeping, and you see a powerful hand, resting atop his head;
That is when you know,
Now is the time for you to let go.

Little Bradley headed back with Lucas to recover Jonas. The pair had made a good score in the liquor store hold up. Little Bradley had to figure out a plan to hold Jonas hostage. Jonas is a little chump. Thought Little Bradley, if pushed he will talk.

Lucas, said Little Bradley, we need to go uptown. We can find a drunk and rent an inexpensive hotel room. We can hold Jonas there until this blows over.

The pair headed uptown. Looking for a safe place, with not a lot of traffic, and with a fire escape to go in and out. The Hotel Yukon" struck a note in little Bradleys' head. Little Bradley and Lucas, stole another car for their escapade..

The two headed for the hotel, they enlisted the help of a wino to rent the room. Once the pair had the keys. They paid the wino twenty dollars, and dumped the stolen car.

Hopping on a bus, the pair rode several blocks. Hopping off the bus. The two hot wired and stole another car. On arrival to the site, where Jonas had been dumped, Jonas had managed to crawl amongst a pile of cardboard boxes. Little Bradley doused Jonas with a cold drink. Little Bradley told Little Jonas."Man, said Little Bradley. To keep from killing you, we have to hold you, until this thing blows over.

Jonas didn't say anything. He just went along with the plan. The boys were friends. I know that it doesn't seem that way; But those boys considered themselves family.

The boys arrived at the hotel. Little Bradley and Lucas took Jonas up the fire escape, through the window. The boys tied Jonas to the bed. Lucas went out for food and a change of clothes for Jonas. Little Bradley stayed with Jonas., letting him shower.

Lucas arrived an hour later, with a change of clothes and burgers and fries, and milkshakes for the trio. The trio had $327.00 from the robbery. No words were exchanged regarding the incident. As little Bradley looked out the window of the hotel. Little Bradley told Lucas that they needed to take off another liquor store before the money ran out.

Lucas and Bradley turned to leave, looking back at Jonas. Jonas' reply was "do what you have to do". The pair left scouting the area for their next hold-up site.

Ebony watched the movers load the last box onto the truck. Ebony had married Derrick and they had two boys and a daughter. The children were grown now. Derk was twenty one years old. The children were grown now. Derk was twenty one years old. And Derrick 11 was 23 years old. Ebonys' daughter, Bonnie was nineteen years old.

Derrick Sr. headed a pharmaceutical company. Derrick was a doctor by profession, who had discovered a very expensive cure for AIDS: Derk was a lawyer and felt inferior to Derrickll, who was a doctor. Derk felt that he had to prove himself to his father in order to win his love and affection. When Derrick 11 was the apple of his fathers' eye. Always vieing for his fathers' love and approval. Bonnie was was away at college. Bonnie was studying to be a chemist.

Ebony sat in her easy chair, thumbing through her photo album. Ebony saw a picture staring at her of Matthias. Matthias and Derrick ll, had been friends through college. Derrickll and Matthias were inseparable at one time. That is until Derrick Sr. saw some potential in Matthias.

Derrick Sr. was going to give Matthias a position at one of his companies. However, Matthias just disappeared one day. Ebony had always suspected Derrickll of foul play.

Hey Matthias, said Derrickll as he put the top down on his convertible. Have you thought about my fathers' offer? Asked Derrickll, as he hopped into his car. I have not yet decided, said Matthias, as he loaded his hunting gear into the trunk of the car. (Derrick11 and Derk, had achieved college at such an early age, due to the fact, that the boys had went to school since they were four years old, all year round. Never a summer vacation, just school for the boys.

Well we are on our way, said Derrickll, as the pair headed for the highway. Derrickll was an outdoorsman. He loved hunting expeditions, camping and fishing.

Derrickll and Matthias had purchases a cabin. The boys spent a lot of time outdoors. The two rose early for their hunting expedition that morning, after a breakfast of eggs and coffee, the boys headed on their way.

The two headed through the brush, when suddenly, Derrickll took his hunting rifle, slamming the butt of the gun down on Mathias' skull. Matthias fell to the ground, looking up at Derrickll in disbelief. Derrickll, took his rifle putting two slugs into Matthias' head. Yelling, you won't work for my father. Derrickll, took a shovel from his car, Derrickll buried Matthias on the hill.

Matthias was reported missing, but he has never been heard

of since that hunting trip. Derrickll, still visits Matthias' grave on the hill and puts flowers upon the gravesite, that Derrickll made for him.

Ebony thought of Derk. Derk was Ebony" out of place son. Full of some, insecurities,, but honest, and hard working. Derk and Derrickll, started at Yale University, two years apart. The boys were younger than most of the other students. The boys were doing well in school.

Ebony had a Masters Degree, in business. Ebony helped to run the companies. Most of the time, right from her own home, via a computer system..

Derk sat studying for his exam. Derrick ll was out on the town, as usual. Hey Seth, said Derrickll, as he walked over to the table where Seth and his date were sitting. Did you do what I asked? Said Derrickll. Seth motioned for his date to leave the table. .Oh, you mean the exams, yes my buddy, said Seth. Come with me. I have them in the trunk of my car.

The two walked out the back door of the club. Seth held out his hand, as Derrickll pulled out two crisp 100.00 bills and handed them to Seth. Seth walked to the parking lot, to his car and opened the trunk. Seth pulled up the floor -board, pulling out two exams. Seth walked over to Derrickll, handing him the two exams.

That night Derrickll went back to Derks' room. Derrickll saw his brother sleeping, with a pile of papers atop him. He had been studying hard. Derrick 11 placed one of the exams atop Derks' stereo system, and left.

Derrickll went to his dorm and peacefully slept. But first Derrickll made a phone call to the campus police. Using an identifiable voice, via his computer system, Derrickll named his brother Derk as the thief who steals exams.

Derk was expelled from school,. Derks father Derrick Sr. pulled some strings to keep Derk in school. Derk could not take the stares and the finger pointing. Derk transferred to a local college. Derk became a lawyer, but he left the profession with his fathers' company and started his own law firm. Derk and his fathers' relationship was strained. Derrick Sr. was always comparing the two boys. Derk had to prove himself to his father somehow, and Derk knew that one day he would.

Ebony came back to reality. Ebony and her family were moving back to Ebonys' hometown to open a new pharmaceutical company. Derrickll was to run the new company. Ebony had went ahead and purchased a mansion.

The mansion was big enough to contain Ebonys' children. Later on, the families of Ebonys' children would live in the mansion. The mansion was perfect

Derrick Sr., would eventually join the family, when the home business matters were taken care of. Ebony dreaded being without Derrick Sr. close to her. Ebony had learned to live with it. When Ebony married into the Brownville family, the women warned Ebony, to learn to live without your man. If you cannot stand the loneliness, we suggest you seek a companion. Ebony, and DerrickSr., had almost been married for twenty- five years. Ebony never had an affair.

The men seemed to accept their women sleeping around. However, if they felt threatened by it, the men just put a stop to the relationship.

The strange man was always there, looking, watching and waiting; The stranger watched from the shadows; Always around, so quiet, hardly making a sound, who was this man? And what did he want. Probably someone my father hired to watch over us, and that is certainly nothing new , said Bonnie to herself. Bonnie was Ebonys' only daughter. Bonnie was going to sneak into town tonight; She had a date with Eddie; Bonnie knew that her family would never approve of Eddie. Eddie was a smooth talker, who couldn't hold down a job. Rumor had it that Eddie sold drugs to live, but Bonnie only saw tall, dark, and handsome Eddie who swept her off her feet.

Naomi, now watch the door and let me know when the lights are out, said Bonnie as she opened the window. Naomi waited for the housemothers to troop down the hall, when the footsteps stopped Naomi knew, they were gone, and the coast was clear.

Finally, Bonnie climbed out the window to the waiting arms of Eddie. Eddie and Bonnie walked to the gate. Eddie helped Bonnie climb the gate. The two headed for Eddies' car, and drove the wide- open road. The two were going to a club where Eddies' friends hung out.. Eddie casually asked Bonnie, "Did your old man send the 3,000.00,? I need it badly baby. Dad cut me off, said Bonnie, he said not another cent until I bring my grades up Well, what am I suppose to do about that, said Eddie, as he pulled over to the side of the road .Now Eddie, said Bonnie, as she put her hands to her face; You promised no more. That was before I knew how stupid you were, said Eddie, as he grabbed Bonnie by the hair. Get out of the car, yelled Eddie. Bonnie inched out of the car and started to run. Bonnie knew to run for safety, once Eddie got that way. Eddie grabbed Bonnie by the hair, hitting her repeatedly, till she fell to the ground. Bonnie could hardly see, as she vaguely saw a figure standing over Eddie, repeatedly kicking him. Bonnie watched the stranger walk over to her and lift her up in his arms, carrying her to a vehicle. The stranger called the school via a car phone and delivered Bonnie to a hospital Emergency room.

After being treated, for cuts and bruises, Bonnie was released to the elder housemother. The stranger had disappeared, vanished. It was as if he had vanished into thin air.

Bonnie knew that she was in trouble with her parents, but who was the stranger?

A NEW GENERATION

Rachel dressed for the ballet, so as to be ready promptly by 7:30; Bret and Rachel had to pick up Ermine and Terrence by 8:00pm, so as to be seated by 8:45. The ballet was to begin by 9:00p.m. Rachel took one last look at herself in the full-length mirror, and did her finishing touches on her nails, when she hear her mother, Menna let Bret in. Menna called for Rachel.

Brets' mouth fell wide open when he envisioned Rachel in a beautiful, black and gold sarong styled gown. Rachels' hair was flowing softly over her shoulders, the beauty from her face sparkled.

Bret walked over to Rachel and handed her a corsage. Menna had the camcorder going. "What a lovely couple you two make said Menna, as she smiled.

Lets' go, said Rachel, as Bret held the door for her. "Did you park in the driveway? Asked Rachel. Huh, said Bret, as he watched Rachel. Rachel and Bret started on their way, to pick up Ermine and Terrence. Ermine and Terrence came out as we were pulling into the driveway. Rachel noticed as Ermine and Terrence got into the car that Ermine seemed a little dazed. Hey girl, what's' going on, said Ermine as she patted Rachels' shoulder.

Ermine is anything wrong, asked Rachel? "I'm just fine, said Ermine; Well ,, lets head for the ballet, said Bret as he turned onto the highway. Rachel could hear Ermine and Terrence bickering in the back seat. Bret asked Terrence, how was the job coming along? It is finally kicking in, replied Terrence.

Terrence was a district attorney; Terrence and Ermine had been dating for three years. They met while at college. Terrence had purchased Irmas' mothers' home. While Irma and her family occupied the mansion after Gerald Sr. came home. Irmas' mom had passed away at 102 years old, and left Irma the house. Irma was a pediatrician. Ermine was following in her mothers' footsteps. Gerald Sr. had been a college professor and a carpenter. Gerald Sr. was wealthy. His father, now deceased was an oil mogul..

The ballet was beautiful, colorful; The dancers looked like figurines, so graceful in their movements. The ballet lasted for two hours. Afterwards we had dinner in the banquet room of the concert hall. The orchestra played mellow and soothing music.

Ermine excused herself to go to the ladies room. Terrence followed behind Ermine. Terrence was trying to get Ermine to open her purse. The two were bickering. Ermine shoved Terrence and proceeded to the ladies room. Terrence came back, clearing his throat and straightening his tie.

Is everything alright, asked Bret? Oh just fine, replied Terrence. Ermine is a little firecracker, said Terrence, as he laughed nervously. Ermine finally came back, really peppy and talkative. Ermine, may I see you on the terrace, said Rachel? Sure, said Ermine as she and Rachel headed for the terrace.

Ermine, what are you on, asked Rachel? I just have a little something once in a while to pick myself up, said Ermine. The job is getting to me. Ermine, said Rachel, I think that you are not being totally honest. I already talked to Aunt Irma. I know what's' going on with you. Let me arrange to get you some help. I am not that bad, said Ermine, I can quit anytime I want..

Do you think I believe that said Rachel? Rachel took hold of both Ermines' shoulders. Ermine look at me , this is Rachel you are talking to, you need help. Can't we discuss this later, said Ermine? (Rachel and her brothers called Irma, Aunt Irma, since they had grown up so closely together, no blood relation). At that moment the maitre de' paged Rachel. (Rachel had left her cell phone along with her purse at the table. Rachel had a phone call). I guess this will have to wait, said Rachel to Ermine, I had better take my phone call. I will be over to talk to you tomorrow at lunch, Ermine I don't want you to lose everything. "Fine, said Ermine, as she walked over to Terrence. Well, I had better take my phone call, said Rachel to herself; I wonder who it could be?

Rachel went over to the front desk. Hello, said Rachel. You had better stay away from Bret, or else, said the voice. Who is this asked Rachel? Why don't you ask Bret who I am, he left me with his child. Left you with his child, said Rachel? That's' what I said, replied the voice, and you will be hearing from me. The phone hung up loudly. What on earth is going on, said Rachel? Bret doesn't have any children.

Rachel went back to the table, with a look of shock on her face. What's' wrong, ,asked Bret? You look as if you've seen a ghost. It was that phone call, said Rachel. If you say so, replied Bret. Ermine and Terrence came back to the table, a little more relaxed with each other. By 12:30 we were ready to end our evening.

Rachel and Bret dropped off Ermine and Terrence, and headed home. On the way to Rachels' house, Rachel told Bret about the phone call. I don't have any children, replied Bret. If you ever get

REFLECTIONS OF LIFE

another phone call like that, please put me on the phone, so that I can clear things up.

That is strange, said Rachel, why would she say such a thing like that? I have no idea, said Bret. Yes, said Rachel, I believe you. Now lets talk about us, and where our relationship is headed. Good topic, replied Bret, smiling. You know Rachel, said Bret, II would marry you in a minute, if you would just say the words. Just be patient with me, said Rachel, I need at least a year to set my life and our childrens' future. But what is preventing us from seeing more of each other, said Rachel. I have been meaning to tell you, that I Have gotten a promotion. The job calls for me to be in town more than usual, I will be able to see you whenever I want to now.

Bret, was now a superior, which meant that he would have men working under him, from his home base. Now Bret would head his own training camp. Why Bret that is wonderful, said Rachel. I guess things are finally working out for us. Brets' title was now Admiral Bret Tyler.

Bret pulled into Rachels' driveway. Rachel noticed that her truck looked a bit lopsided. Rachel got out of the car and walked over to her truck. Rachels' two passenger side tires had been slashed. Bret examined the truck. Bret phoned the road service from his car. What on earth is going on, said Rachel. First that phone call, now this. Do you think that I should phone for the police and file a report, asked Rachel? Sweetheart you just go inside, and I will handle everything, said Bret. Rachel and Bret kissed tenderly. Rachel went inside and showered. Afterwards, Rachel thought about the nights events.. (Rachel heard a voice say, trust in bret.)

Rachel drifted off to sleep, only to be awakened by the ringing of the phone at 4am. Hello, said Rachel, sleepily. Hello dear; Grandma is this you, asked Rachel? Yes dear, we have a family emergency. Its' your grandfather dear.He was rushed to the hospital, its his heart. I am not quite sure that he will pull through this time. Please tell David and Menna to meet me at the hospital. Rachel quickly hung up and ran to wake her parents.

Menna and David went to Saint Josephs' Hospital David and Menna looked at David Sr. lying there, looking so frail. Frances, Davids' mother,sat at the head of Davids' fathers' bed. David Sr. reached out for Davids' hand. Menna stood on the opposite side of David, looking on in silence.. David Sr. nodded to his wife Frances. (Davids' mother).

Frances had a brief case with her. Davidll, father was a successful business executive. He owned JOHNUP Pharmaceuticals. David Sr. had expanded the business to four other cities. There were two companies overseas. That totaled six companies in all. David ll had overseen these companies while he was over seas.. In the military. David had started these two companies from scratch.

Menna and David, said Frances, inside this brief case is all the important documents that you will need to know about the family businesses. Ownership is hereby transferred to David and Menna Phillips and family. Mark Rachel, and Chad, Matthew. MAY GOD BE WITH YOU.

David Sr. squeezed Davids' and Mennas' hand and closed his eyes.. The cardiac monitor let out a long humming sound. Doctors, and nurses rushed to David Sr. side, trying to revive him, working feverishly. The children finally arrived to witness this. After working for over an hour on David Sr. he was pronounced dead.

David fled from the room, tears flooding his eyes. Eventhough, he knew that dads' day would come soon, that did not make it any easier.. Menna went after David. David said to Menna. "Dad is gone, as David 11 sat in a chair in the hallway of the hospital. Menna stood in front of David and held him close to her abdomen. David cried like a baby at the hospital that night. David refused the sedative that the doctors' had ordered for him. Menna and David, sat at the hospital until the sun came up.

The funeral was a saddening event. The family seemed physically and emotionally drained and exhausted. Everyone was so mechanical. Everyone going through the motions, but numb on the inside. The family did keep their composure, but the tears flowed freely.

For six months, David ll, mourned the death of his father. Davidll was lost, he half ate, did not sleep, and barely got out of bed. David ll was having a hard time accepting his fathers' death.

David knew that one day the responsibility of the business would be his. Just as it was his grandfathers., And his father before that. The business went back for four generations. David ll would be the fifth generation to take over this billon - dollar empire, that his forefathers had built. Menna knew that David would do right by his father.

SIX MONTHS LATER

One morning Menna woke up. David was not in bed. Menna got out of bed and noticed the light on in Davids' study. Menna gently pushed the half open door, there she saw David at his desk. David was going over the companies documents. Menna gently pulled the door closed and went to the kitchen for a cup of Emmas' coffee.

She stood on the street corner, waiting for her john to pick her up. She had previously registered at a sleezy motel, on the outskirts of town. As she and the strange man she had picked up headed for the motel. The young woman pulled out the keys to the room.

The woman, opened the motel room door and let the stranger enter first. The man went to the rest room to freshen up. The man came out and the woman of the night was laid out nude on the bed. The woman got up and did a suggestive dance. The stranger hungrily watched as the woman sauntered over to him. The two became one.

The woman quietly reached over the side of the bed. She reached into a pouch. The woman had previously planted the gun and pouch on the underside of the bed. The woman pulled out the gun, putting the gun, ever so quietly, to the back of the strangers' head. The woman squeezed the trigger. The stranger was twice shot in the head.

The man slumped over the woman. The woman pushed the man away. Took the sheet off the bed and spread the sheet out flat on the floor. The woman placed the body onto the sheet. She dragged the body down the deserted hallway of the motel. The body was wrapped carefully, and the woman hoped that no one would come. In that part of town nobody cared anyway. The woman dragged the body out the back exit door, and to the strangers car. The woman lifted the body into the owners' car. The woman got into the car and drove the body to a nearby field. The woman dumped the body into a ditch. She burned the car, pushing the vehicle over a cliff. The woman walked down the dirt road, saying to herself. The next tim I will leave the body at the hotel. Dionna smiled to herself, dead bodies are just to much trouble to dispose of.

Dionna halted a taxi, and headed on her way home. Mrs Krenshaw was asleep in her easy chair. She had fell asleep reading. Dionna took off her shoes and tipped up the stairs. Dionna got into the shower. Dionna scrubbed herself so hard that she noticed her skin was burning.

Dionna got out of the shower. She went to her daughters' room and kissed her goodnight. Dionna went back to her room, and climbed into bed. Dionna reached for her teddy bear, stuck her thumb in her mouth and drifted off to sleep.

CHARLOTTES AFFLICTION

Lets' take my car, said Menna as she and Anna headed out the door. Did you let Collette know that we were coming, said Anna? I left a message on Collettes' answering machine, said Menna. Menna unlocked the car door. The two got into the car and proceeded to drive to Collettes house. Anna and Menna rang the doorbell. Collette took a while to get to the door. Collette slowly opened the door. Collette, its' us, said Anna, let me in.

We heard yelling and screaming coming from the upper part of the house. Collette, said Menna, what is going on? Its' Charlotte, said Collette, she is addicted to heroine. Right now she is going through a withdrawal. Collette, said Anna, is there anything that we can do? Anna, please ask Jerrod to be on stand by, said Collette. Menna I have to go to work in an hour. I hate to ask you to do this, but could you please stay with Charlotte. Sure, said Menna, I will stay the second four hours, said Anna. Thanks both of you, said Collette. Just leave her be. I borrowed a straight jacket, said Collette, Charlotte is in restraint, so that she cannot hurt herself. I will call home every hour that I possibly can, said Collette.Collette left for work. Anna went to Jerrods' home office to brief him as to what was going on. Menna took out her bible and went to Charlottes' room.

Menna sat there in a rocking chair next to Charlottes' bed and closed her eyes. Charlotte was not recognizable. Her lips were chapped, her hair was in disarray; Her eyes were a yellowed color. Charlotte did not look like herself at all. As Menna closed her eyes, she prayed to herself. Menna asked God to pull Collette through this. Menna asked God for strength and guidance. Menna asked God to sharpen Charlottes' senses and please make her stronger to resist the Devils' tool, so as not to stumble again. Menna sat there in the rocking chair praying to herself for thirty minutes. Menna finally opened her bible to the book of JOB. Menna began to read JOB aloud. Charlotte, who was restrained to the bed, continued to wiggle, and squirm trying to free herself. Menna continued to read JOB louder and louder. Charlotte began to vomit. Twenty minutes later Charlotte fell into a deep sleep.

Menna found herself dozing off as she sponged Charlottes' head off and cleaned her up (Menna wore disposable gloves throughout the ordeal).

Menna saw a cloud hover over Charlottes' bed. It was a gray cloud. The cloud was in Charlottes' head area. Menna saw a huge hand with a shackle on it. The hand was holding that huge sword. The sword began to raise higher and higher and then it started to come down at Charlottes' throat Menna yelled out NO! All of a sudden a hand even much bigger and more powerful, reached out from out of nowhere. The most powerful arm and hand was wearing an open shackle, on its' wrist. The Powerful arm reached up and grabbed the sword-wielding arm. Like a puff of smoke the gray cloud came and vanished the sword- wielding arm. Menna raised her head, for Menna had been facing downward; Menna looked at Charlotte. Charlotte had a glow and was sleeping peacefully,. She was smiling. Charlotte looked like an innocent angelic child.

Menna brushed Charlottes' hair and burned the contamination, in a fireplace in Charlottes room. At that moment the room filled with a golden light and remained there. Menna quietly left the room. 'THANK YOU MY HEAVENLY FATHER, said Menna. Just then the doorbell rang, MENNA SAID AMEN, AND HEADED TO ANSWER THE DOOR.

JERROD AND ANNA ARRIVE

There stood Anna and Jerrod to relieve Menna. Menna was drained and didn't want to talk. Menna got her car keys from Anna, and hurried out the door. Menna did not feel like answering any questions. The voice said, everything will be alright words are not necessary, seeing is believing.

Jerrod went to check Charlotte, and stood at the opened door of the room in disbelief. Anna said Jerrod, I thought that this withdrawal has only been in progress since this morning. As far as I know, replied Anna. That is correct. Anna let out a sigh of relief, for Anna knew what had taken place. Anna was living proof.

Jerrod went to check Charlotte for the last time. Jerrod examined Charlottes' arms and legs. They were badly scarred from the needle. Jerrod called for Anna and made a list of the things that he needed from the office to perform the skin graft. Jerrod could complete the surgery in less than an hour.

Anna arrived forty-five minutes later with the things that Jerrod needed to do the corrective surgery. Jerrod worked on Anna until the scars were no longer visible. Jerrod did not use any drugs, he used an ectopic numbing solution. Charlotte was to exhausted to even realize what was going on. Charlotte felt a little pain, but for the most part the surgery went well.

Jerrod wrapped Charlottes' legs and arms. Jerrod gave Charlotte a mild analgesic and left the room.

How is she , asked Anna. Anna replied Jerrod, I don't believe in miracles. But this day has just changed my mind. This recovery was a miraculous one. And truly a miracle. Charlotte is as good as new, when the scar tissue heals, there will be no evidence of drug use.

Anna and Jerrod waited for Collette to arrive. When Collette finally arrived at Twelve midnight, Jerrod was out in the car waiting for Anna. Anna did not want to discuss it. Jerrod did the corrective surgery on Charlottes' arms and legs. He did a skin graft. Instructions are on the table and the scar tissue should heal in two weeks. Your mail is on the table, said Anna, as she closed the door behind her. Anna headed for Jerrods' and her car. Some things are just better not discussed.

There was a letter for Charlotte amongst the pile. Months ago, Charlotte had applied for several positions for a journalist position, and related jobs. Charlotte had applied for a talk show position. The letter was from CBS.

In Charlottes present condition, I doubt that this position will do her any good now, said Collette to herself. Collette stuffed the letter into her pocket. Charlotte had applied for this position sometime ago. Charlotte had a Masters Degree in journalism. What a waste, said Collette to herself, as she headed for Charlottes' room.

Collette opened Charlottes' bedroom door: Collettes' heart practically dropped to her feet; Charlotte was sitting up in bed, writing in her journal. Collette slowly walked over to Charlotte touching her, as if she was trying to see if she was real or was this just a dream. Charlotte looked like and angel, there was a gold glow to her room. Except for the bandages, Charlotte looked beautiful to Collette. Charlotte looked like the daughter that Collette had known.

Hello mother, said Charlotte, how did work go tonight? (Collette stared at Charlotte dumbfoundly. You see Charlotte had never asked Collette about her job before. Just fine dear, said Collette. I have a letter for you, said Collette. Colllette handed Charlotte her mail. Charlotte stared at the letter in disbelief. Charlotte ripped open the envelope.

Collette ran downstairs to phone Menna. Collette did not even give Menna a chance to say hello, before she said , Menna? Yes, said Menna; Its' Charlotte, what did you do, she is healed, she is so peaceful. The atmosphere, what happened? Collette, everything is alright, just calm down and know that Charlotte is going to be fine.

Now if only Charlene would come home, said Collette. Charlene has been gone for almost a week. What! Said Menna. All of a sudden Charlotte let out a scream, Collette said, Collette, said Menna , I will call you back.

What is it said Collette: Momma I got the talk show host job: Oh Charlotte that is wonderful, said Collette :Collette hugged

Charlotte.

Collette came in from work that night. Collette walked up the stairs to Charlottes' room, and behold, Charlotte was going through her closet, trying on clothes. Charlotte was looking for the perfect outfit for her second interview. Collette quietly closed the door, saying to herself, "now that's the Charlotte that I remember".

Tess and Terry seated themselves on the ottoman; Terry said Tess, I think now you are old enough to know. With all of these occurrences, throughout the years you need to know everything. Tess told Terry about her sordid life. About the shelter murders, the anonymous packages, and finally who the cuff links belonged to. Tess told Terry about her conception. Tess and Terry talked for at least two hours., going over everything.

Tess looked at her mother and said, "Momma, I know, I know everything. I don't understand, replied Tess. How do you know? I have known for a very long time. You see momma, Menna kept journals. Menna talked to me when you were ill. This came about because of the shelter murders. I have been turning these things over in my mind, and I wish to commend you for your strength and loyalty. When I was away at school, my first reaction.was one of anger. It wasn't your fault . I am just relieved that it is all out in the open. The two embraced and all of a sudden Tess knew that she and Terry would be alright.

JOSEPH

Joseph got off the plane, he was now in Nevade, now to get to the place where Terry was held hostage. Joseph rented a car and went to the Nevada officials to get the exact location of the place. The officials were cooperative. Joseph was given an escort to the location. Joseph pulled up in front of the run down shack. Joseph went inside. The place looked like something out of a horror movie. There were gruesome pictures covering the wall. Pictures of women with body parts severed. There was a terrible odor to the place, and flies were everywhere. Joseph went outside for air. On entering again, this time wearing a face mask and gloves, Joseph went through the contents of the closets. Most of the things were being held for evidence. Joseph noticed a hallowed spot in the floor board. Joseph found pictures and letters.

Joseph gathered up the contents, and went outside to go over the material. Joseph saw that these letters were letters that the killer had written. The letters were letters that the killer had written to himself. Joseph started to read, starting with the last letter first. Joseph saw what only a sick mind could write. These letter must have been written just before each killing.

There were detail to detail accounts of how the killer severed the bodies, and also how he planned to murder Terry and Tess. Joseph needed some answers. It seemed as if someone was trying to cover for this killer. The killer was in Josephs' hometown.

Joseph went to the Nevada officials and asked why these letters had not been confiscated? Joseph found out that the killer was the son of the captain. Joseph talked to the captain and was given a detailed description of the man he was looking for.

Joseph chartered a plane. The plane ride home was a long and restless one. Joseph called the home office. Joseph called to make sure that officials were guarding his family to be. The men were at their stations, Joseph carried a cellular phone.

Several hours later Joseph arrived home, he did not go straight to Tess and Terry. He checked with the other officials who were assigned to the case, on the well-being of Tess and Terry.

JOSEPH NEEDED TO SHOWER AND SHAVE; He had planned to ask Tess to marry him.

Tess and Terry sat at the dining room table playing dominoes. Tess felt a draft. Terry did you leave a window open, asked Tess? Tess went to check the windows. No, momma, said Terr. Tess checked the windows and noticed that the side door was ajar. Tess went to close the door. Tess turned to walk away, and there it was then that the man grabbed Tess and covered her mouth. It reminded Tess of how similar it was to that nightmarish night when she was raped.

The man forced Tess to the basement of the house. Momma, called Terry, as she walked down the basement stairs. The basement was a big dark place. Momma, where are you, said Terry. Terry reached for the light switch. The light bulb was gone. Terry walked the length of the basement, looking for Tess. Terry heard muffled sounds, and then she heard something crash to the concrete Floor.

Joseph checked his messages, there was a message from Dr. Gayle, a plastic surgeon. The message said; (Confessed serial killer going by the name of John Doe. Tess and Terry are in grave danger, please confirm); Oh God, said Joseph, Tess and Terry are in trouble, the killer had plastic surgery, which means the undercover agents could not identify him. Joseph hurriedly left running for his car. Joseph picked up his car radio to alert agents. The wires had been tampered with. The radio was dead. Joseph realized that his phone was inside the house. Joseph ran to a neighbors home, the neighbor was outdoors watering. Joseph yelled, I have to use your phone. Haven't you heard, said Mrs. Garrett? The phone lines are down. Joseph' face became flushed.

REFLECTIONS OF LIFE

Joseph ran for his car. Joseph started the car, it was dead. Joseph started on foot. Joseph headed for traffic, since it would be easier for him to flag down a citizen for the loan of his or her car. No one seemed to want to stop. Joseph headed for a traffic light. Joseph ran up to the fist car at the light. Joseph jumped into the car,letting the driver out, after ahowing him his badge. Joseph headed to Tess and Terrys' home. Five blocks ahead, and the car ran out of gas. With about a mile to go Joseph started running. There were other cars, other lights, but somehow Joseph decided to rely on himself.

Terry looked over at a pile of unused insulation. Terry walked slowly toward the pile. All of a sudden a man jumped out with Tess being held at gunpoint Tess said, Terry, please be calm, run Terry, save yourself, said Tess. No momma, yelled Terry, I won't, I won't leave you. The stranger pushed Tess into Terry, Telling them both to sit on the concrete floor, back to back. He held the gun on them. Now I got you, said the stranger, all that time behind bars, because of you, retorted the stranger.That night, I came back to the college, I came back for you Tess. Only that girl who came to the door, she just kept screaming, she wouldn't be quiet Shut up I yelled, but she just kept screaming. I tried to quiet her , I just kept choking her, harder and harder until I could no longer hear the scream.

I ran out onto the grounds, the police were there, I was caught by the police. I put up a fight but was subdued in spite of my efforts to escape. Now you took my life, and now I am going to take yours. The man cocked his gun, and Terry yelled, daddy don't. The man stared wide-eyed at Terry. I am your daughter. The man stood there frozen to his spot. That night, remember, you and momma, daddy its' me Terry.

The killer dropped his hands to his sides. "Yes repeated Terry, your daughter. The killer looked confused. He started to laugh, a horrid frightful laugh. Finally quieting down, the stranger said, then we are all one, this means that we all must die as one. The killer raised his gun once more, Tess slowly walked towards the killer. Take my life, said Tess, but let our daughter live. You stay back the killer warned. Daddy the cuff links. I have your cuff links. Don't you remember, said Terry? Terry knew that she had to do something. Daddy why do you want to kill your family, said Terry? I don't replied the killer as he once again lowered his gun.

While the stranger was in the process of loading his gun, Terry darted for the stranger, jump kicking the gun from his hand. Terry kicked the gun away from the killer. Tess and Terry turned to run out the door. The killer ran to recover the gun. When he recovered the gun, Joseph burst into the door, firing his gun into the killer, until he could fire no more. The killer fell to the concrete floor.

Joseph went over to check the body. Kicking the gun away from the killer. Joseph walked over to Tess and Terry. Tess saw the killer stand up. Joseph had his back turned away from the killer., as the killer reached for Josephs' neck, Tess dived onto the floor, picking up the killers gun, Tess fired the gun until she could fire no more.

As the trio walked up the basement stairs, Joseph said "Tess will you marry me"? Yes, I will Tess replied. Terry, Tess and Joseph walked out the door as the backup crew arrived. What a day said Joseph as he hugged Terry and Tess.

Mark hopped into his red convertible and headed for Angelas' house. Mark should be able to make it to Angelas' house in a little over forty five minutes. Mark and Angela had become friends during college. Angela and Geraldll were seeing each other at that time. Gerald ll and Angela were married shortly after college graduation.

Geraldll and Angela lived in a secluded area, away from friends. Mark had not been in touch with Geraldll and Angela since they lived so far. Both of their jobs kept them out of town a lot.

Mark turned into traffic and heard the screeching of tires. Mark realized that his car had been hit. Mark put on his courtesy lights and pulled over to the side of the road. The young woman stepped from the car. She was beautiful, thought Mark as she walked over to him. Hello, my name is Barbara Houston, said the young woman, here is my insurance card. I must apologize for my negligence. Accidents will happen, said Mark. I am not always so forward, said Tatata, what do you do Mark, asked Tarara. That's' not important, said Mark, but I am self-employed. Doctor Houston, said Mark as he handed the young woman back her insurance card? Not quite replied Tarara, in about six more months. The two exchanged phone numbers, and Mark asked Tarara out for a date, that following Friday. Mark hopped into his convertible, and headed for Angelas' house.

Mark arrived to Angelas' house, and rang the doorbell. Hello Mr. Phillips, said Ava: the housekeeper after she opened the door. Mark could hear Angela sobbing through the opened door..

Please come in Mr. Phillips, said Eva. Hello Eva , said Mark. How long has Angela been like this? All day replied Eva, as she took Marks' hat and coat.

Mark made his way to where Angela was, in her studio. Angela what's' wrong, said Mark? Its' Geraldll, he never comes home anymore. And when he is home, he just sits in his study, talking out of his head. His job called, Geraldll has not been to work in weeks.

No one has heard from him. That's' strange, said Mark How long has it been since you heard from Geraldll. About a week ago, said Angela. He ran out of here like a madman, and I haven't seen, or heard from him since. I am thinking about hiring an investigator. Not yet, said Mark, let me see qhat I can come up with. If Geraldll is in town, I will find him. Angela, said Mark, I don't want you to worry, I will be in touch.

Do you think that you will be alright, or would you like for Rachel to stay with you a couple of days. I will be alright, sighed Angela, as she continued molding her clay figurine. Angela, said Mark, as he held her chin in his hand. Look at me. Angela looked up at Mark, red eyed. Everything is going to be alright. Mark gave Angela a friendly hug. Have faith, we will find him. Mark turned to leave, he rang for Eva. Eva came in. My hat and coat please, said Mark, Sure Mr. Phillips, replied Eva. Mark called Angela. Mark turned to look at Angela. Thank you, said Angela. Mark put on his hat and coat, went up to see the twins and left.

Mark was very upset with Geraldll at that moment. Hark had been best man at Geraldll' wedding. I will find him, said Mark to himself. And he had better have a good explanation, or I am going to beat the tar out of him. Mark climbed into his convertible, and pulled onto the dirt road, heading home.

Geraldll sat in the hallway of the tenement; I have to find a hideout, thought Geraldll to himself, they are closing in on me. Geraldll needed a bath and a shave. But the devil had taken over his mind, and Geraldll was not thinking rationally.

Geraldll saw a rat, Geraldll followed the rat with his eyes. Geraldll watched the rat, run into a dirt field. Geraldll followed the rat with his eyes. Geraldll watched the rat disappear into the sewer. Geraldll ran to the dirt field and found the manhole sewer cover. Geraldll found a stick and took the lid up, Geraldll went down into the sewer, looking around him. Geraldll had found his hiding place. Geraldll needed supplied, he had his credit card. Geraldll purchased needed supplies. Geraldll purchased a kerosene lamp, a sleeping bag, a warm jacket, boots, canned goods, a shot gun, and a battery operated transistor radio, and

Matches. Now they won't ever find me, mumbled Gerald ll under his breath.

Geraldll took his supplies underground and there Gerald ll took up residency. Geraldll, waited for the sun to go down, he had to gather some rocks to build him a stove. Geraldll went via the manhole cover, looking around that dirt field.

Geraldll noticed a pile of dirt at a higher level than the rest of the piles. Geraldll went over to the pile. Large rocks were buried in that pile. Geraldll started to dig with a shovel, he had purchased. Geraldll removed more dirt, noticing that it was a woman. Geraldll uncovered the body, he stared in disbelief. Geraldll knew this woman. Charlene, Geraldll said, shaking her. (Charlene is Collettes missing daughter). Geraldll removed the remainder of the dirt, lifting Charlene up in his arms. Geraldll lowered Charlene into the sewer, along with himself.

Menna left to pick up Anna. Menna and Anna had planned to go and visit Katherine. Menna had not seen Katherine in months.Menna wondered how Katy and Bradley were doing. Menna pulled up in front of Annas' house. Menna began to blow the horn.Menna had to call for Anna via intercom at the front gate. Ten minutes later Anna appeared. Hi girl, said Menna. How are things going with you? Okay, I guess,replied Anna. Jerrod has something that he wants to share with me. He did not tell me what it was regarding. Only that now is the time for me to know about his weekend disappearances. Well, I guess that is a load off your mind, said Menna. Have you talked to Katherine. These days, said Anna, Katherine is a hard person to catch. I made an appointment to see her this time. Since Katherine has expanded her business (catering Service), she is never home. She rarely returns phone calls or messages. Well, said Menna, diary of a busy woman. I guess, Menna and Anna went to Katherines' second place of business.

When the duo arrived at Katherines' catering service, Katherine was busy. Hi Kathy, said Menna. How are things going with you and the children? Katherine continued working. I cannot talk about it right now, said Katherine. Anna stepped in front of Katherine grabbing her two shoulders. Turning Katherine to face her. Katherine, said Anna, talk to us, stop and talk to us right now. Oh Katherine said, breaking down in tears, my children, I know that I am going to lose them.

They are on the wrong path, and I keep asking myself. "Where did I go wrong?" Katherine, said Menna, we are going to have to grab them and set them on the right track, that's' all. We can repair the damages, things can and will be alright.

Where are the children, asked Menna? I don't know, I haven't seen Bradley in two weeks, and Katy, runs around with the wrong crowd. The children are rebelling. 'Both children are suppose to be working with me after school. They say that they will be here and they never show up, said Katherine. Katy does go to school. But Little Bradley is out of control. whined Katherine.

Well Katherine, said Menna, I guess we have a job to do. We are going to call a meeting with the children. Chad and Rachel will stick close to them. "They probably won't even show up, said Katherine. Then we will send the fathers to get them. I will be in touch with you Katherine, said Menn. Let me set up a date and time with Chad and Rachel, I don't know their schedule.

Anna and Menna turned to leave. Katherine was overwhelmed. That Anna and Menna came to her aid. God must have heard Katherines' pleas for help. Thank you God, said Katherine, as she watched Anna and Menna pull off, waving to them. Katherine felt hopeful once again.

Rachel came inform work. Rachel had Ermine on her mind all day. Rachel had decided to transfer to a college closer to home. That way it would be easier for Rachel to finish her externship. Since Rachel was in her hometown externship program. Rachel would be starting her next semester at home. Rachel had to go back to her college town in California and have her belongings shipped home. Rachel dreaded the move. Bret had offered to accompany Rachel. Bret had a private plane. This was quite convenient for Rachel. Rachel and Bret were to leave that Saturday morning.

Rachel phoned Ermine. But Ermine had not been heard from. Maybe she went back to school, said Rachel. Irma asked Rachel to contact her is she heard from Ermine. Rachel agreed to do so.

ERMINES' FATE

After arriving to the furnished off campus apartment, Rachel and Bret entered the building. The apartment was in a mess. Things were thrown around the apartnebt, and broken. Tachel thought that the apartment had been burglarized. Bret cautioned Rachel not to enter the apartment. Bret went in and looked around. In Ermines' room, Bret saw Ermine passed out on the floor. Bret called Rachel. Please come here. Rachel went to Ermines' room, it was there that Rachel saw Ermine in that state.

Rachel ran over to Ermine. Ermine was unconscious. Ermine had taken something, her pupils were dialated, there was a container next to Ermine, filled with various colors of pills. Ermine had taken an overdose. Bret phoned for an ambulance and Rachel and Bret got Ermine up and started to walk her around, until the paramedics arrived. Rachel called out Ermines' name, trying to bring her to. Rachel heard a sigh come from Ermines' throat. Ermine screamed Rachel. Finally the paramedics arrived. They pumped Ermines' stomach. However, Ermine had to remain in the hospital for three days for observation. Rachel made arrangements with her mother Menna, to have Ermine admitted to Hillcrest Rehabilitation Center program.

After arriving to the center, via Ermines' car, Rachel stayed with Ermine. Bret went back to the apartment to pack and call Irma. Bret had helped Rachel move in, so Bret was familiar with the contents.

Ermine, said Rachel, I have made arrangements with momma for you to be admitted to Hillcrest. Will you agree to that? Anything is better than this, said Ermine. Oh my head is killing me, said Ermine. That was a close call, Ermine, which could have cost you your life. You have got to start placing some type of value on your life, or you are lost. Let me help you through this Ermine. I want my old Ermine back. The Ermine that, I know and love. Bret and me will wait for you to recover and take you back home with us.

Well, I have got to go and get a start helping Bret pack. Aren't you going to ask me why? Asked Ermine. No,, not this time, said Rachel. I look forward to seeing you conquer this problem. Then we can continue on, the way we were. Just agreeing to seek help is reward enough for me. The only thing that matters is you and your future that is the important thing.

ERMINE

Ermine you are ill; But in time your wounds
Will heal; The standards that you set, may be
A bit to high. But Ermine' you can make it; All
You have to do is try.

And in that future life of yours; I wish you well;
I pray that when the eagle soars; And just as the
Lion roars; Your life will be filled with happiness.
That life you chose to restore.

Vanessa Lockwood for a
(A careful life).

Mennas' eyes were really tired. Menna had been working in the companies banks all day. Via a lotus computer. Menna had balanced out with the total profits. Totaling twenty million dollars.

Menna and her family decided to move into the mansion, that way everyone would not be so scattered, here and there. The realtor had found a buyer for their house.

Davids' mom refused to move out of the mansion. I guess she felt closer to her memories there. Maybe the pain would be easier for her to bear with the family around.

Menna noted the time, it was 10:30, Menna was tired. Since the business transfer, Menna had been keeping abreast of the books, and handling Davids' properties business. Menna was busy all the time.

Menna showered and went straight to bed. Menna had an Apple Computer at home that she worked on. Every spare minute she had. Menna was constantly trying to make things better for her family and the employees Mennas' dedication was insurmountable.

Menna was barely asleep, when she saw a faceless figure, in a long flowing powder blue robe. The figure was at the foot of Mennas' bed. Menna reached over for David, but Menna remembered that David was out of town, along with the boys. Menna saw the figure get closer to her. Finally reaching down and touching her. Only Menna could not feel being touched. Menna only felt a cool soothing breeze. Menna looked like her. When the face was finally visible. Menna felt her body become numb. Menna could not feel. Menna saw her spirit self leave her body.

Menna saw herself at Anna and Jerrods' house. Anna and Jerrod were grief stricken. Menna could read it in their faces. Menna saw Anna and Jerrod studying a picture of Taska. Anna and Jerrod missed Taska.

Menna saw Anna and Jerrods' picture vanish from her. Menna saw a picture form of a beautiful desert looking scenario. As Mennas' eyes traveled the length of the desert, something was coming at her real fast. Some type of ranch. Menna saw faces of all types of men. They had a shower of money raining down upon them.. Menna saw a picture, it was a quick picture of Taska., flash across that desert sky. With her hands and feet shackled, Menna saw the money vanish from the picture of those numerous men. Then at that moment, money started to rain on Taska. Taska was restrained. But her mouth was crying out for help. Taska looked fearful. Menna saw oil wells and horses.

Sounds started to come from Mennas' throat, as she decided to try and reach Taska, but Taska just kept moving farther and farther. Away from Menna. Menna sat up quickly and realized that she was in bed. Menna was sweating profusely. Mennas' hands had a black residue on them. Menna could smell oil. Oh God, said Menna. Texas, Taska is in trouble.

Menna knew what had to be done. Menna prayed "Dear God, you have let me know that Taska was in deep trouble. Please God, don't let me be to late. Please guide me and direct me, and see me through this. I know I need proof to call in authorities. I ask you to be with me. Just then Menna heard a voice say. Grandeville Oil Refinery. Menna knew where Taska was being held at that moment. Menna would be in Texas in two weeks for Employee training at one of the families offices. Menna knew that her job was cut out for her. God please be with me.

Two weeks is a long time, I had better get myself there as soon as possible thought Menna to herself. An emergency trip was in order.

ALLANS WOES

Allan readied himself to go to the hospital, that morning to see Cecilia. Allan did not know how long the pain would last. After finding out about Cecilia, his wife. Allan could not think about divorce, just yet. Allan knew that forgiving Cil would be hard.

Cecilia had miscarried. Allan thought about how he felt, when he lost his mother. It did not matter that this child was unborn. The pain still remains the same.

On that drive to the hospital., Allan dreaded to face Cecilia, what was he suppose to say? When arriving to the hospital, Allan checked in at the front desk. Oh you are here for Cecilia, didn't you get our message? Asked the nurse. "Allans' heart began to quicken, what message, asked Allan? Your wife, she signed herself out of the hospital. What? Said Allan. Yes she was gone this morning when the day nurse went to check her vitals. "Any idea where she might have gone? Asked Allan. Did cil leave any message for me? Nothing, replied the nurse, she just left. Thank you, replied Allan,as he headed for Cecilias' room. When arriving to Cecilias' room, Allan sat in the chair. Allan thought of Cecilias' unhappiness throughout the years, nothing seemed to please Cecilia. Cecilia was addicted to amphetamines and had secretly been a call girl, Allan found out.

Allan knew that Cecilia needed psychiatric help. The police had been notified. Allan started packing Cecilias' things. Allan left the hospital with his head hanging down. Allan had lost his whole family. Allan was deeply saddened. Allan would find Cecilia and make her well. Cecilia had always been a beautiful woman, now with her face disfigured, as it was, Allan knew that it was really hard on Cecilia. Allans' mother had passed on but Cecilia was alive somewhere. Allan needed desperately to believe that.

When Menna walked in she noticed that Mark and David were in the study going over some secret plans for the company. It seems that Mark had invented a tampering device. The device was to be added to all companies.

You see in the past David Sr"God rest his soul", had problems with rival companies , which was headed by Ebonys' husband. Now with the tampering device, even if the company was infiltrated, with constant monitoring and surveillance; it would not inter-

REFLECTIONS OF LIFE

fere with production, or company operations. With this device company secrets would remain company secrets. David and Mark were going over a more sophisticated electronical layout to protect the company on a twenty four hour basis, rather than just work hours.

Menna was to be going to Texas in a few short days to educate approved employees. Those who had passed the company dedication tests. David and Mark and Menna had worked on these tests for months. A lot of employees were let go. But Menna had coordinated several classes to educate acceptable employees. The bottom line is, to take care of your employees and your employees will take care of you.

The Employees would be paid for their time. The companies had showed a favorable profit times five companies the figures reached over a billion dollars, and still climbing. The companies were making and saving by recycling their own products Those figures had not been computed as of yet. The end of the year was the time for that. The figures usually matched the companies figures, which means that the figures given X2.

The employees were paid for their time and given a waiver to sign, so as not to bring any law suits against companies. The company would foot the bill if families chose to come to Texas. The two week living expenses would be provided by the company.

Menna still had that uneasy feeling, Menna felt that she needed to meditate to find out if the trip that she and her family would be taking would be safe. There had to be a reason for the way Menna felt.

That night Menna sat in the twins room. Menna looked up to the heavens, and asked : God, said Menna , there is something troubling me. I need you to set my mind at ease. I do not know if this is an ideal time to be taking a trip. Dear God, please advise. AMEN.

That night, Menna had a dream. Menna saw the grandparents along with Mark and Rachel, having a wonderful time at Disneyworld. Menna Menna saw Dionna calling out to her for help. And there were green lights flashing on and off, all over the place. Menna woke up, and sat up in bed,going over her dream.

At that moment Menna felt a cool breath from head to toe. It wasn't a cold wind, it was more like a breeze, or something. Menna saw herself gliding across a dance floor, dressed in a beautiful gown . Menna was looking into Davids' eyes, everything was just so beautiful. So peaceful and soothing.Menna whispered, thank you, and at that moment Menna knew that the trips were still on..

BUFFALO MY HOME

Buffalo is my home;
A place of care and concern
Where the childrens' laughter can
Always be heard;
A feel of song and dance in the air,
Let everyone know we care.

A family that is what we are;
Always near, Yet never far;
A problem is a problem, we all
Pitch in and solve;
An atmosphere, of love. A love which
Knows no bounds.

The lives we lead are simple ones;
But rich we know we are by far;
As the sun comes down and glistens;
On our storybook wonderland;
That is the time we all know;
What a glorious city we live in;
A city called Buffalo.

THE END

THE BEGINNING

Families were expected to buy their own plane tickets at company rates. Menna felt that for safety of the families it was best that families not be separated at this time. The rival company dealt treacherously. So we felt that we were obligated to protect the families.

The billion dollar plan would be profitable to the Phillips' companies. Other companies were already placing orders, for the new electronics system. Now as it stood, in two years, our companies worth would be 10x its' worth now. A lot of work is involved, said Menna. But we can do it.

DERRICKll And IRENE

Derrickll picked up the phone and dialed Irene. Irene was Irmas' twenty one year old daughter. Irene had two years of college left before she would be a certified pediatrician.

Hello, said Irma; Hello, Mrs Brown; This is Derrickll; Derrickll

Brownville; May I please speak to Irene? Irma called Irene to the phone via the intercom. (O lord, said Irma to herself, what on earth could those two be up to now?) Irene was working in the lab. Hello, said Irene, seconds later. Derrickll and Irene had been dating for about a year. Irene would you have dinner with me tonight? Say, I pick you up at 8:00 p.m.

I will be ready replied Irene. See you then, replied Derrickll, as he hung up the phone. Irene rang Irma, via the intercom to let her know that she would not be home for dinner. Irma was a pediatrician. Irma was still in her office working. Irma had three patients left.

Derk walked in the door of the mansion at that moment; Derk checked the messages, and went to check to see who was at home in the mansion besides him. Derk ranged for one of the servants. Josiah the butler appeared. Josiah, said Derk, who is in the mansion besides me? Derrickll is in the study, Mr. Brownville, said Josiah.

Derk made his way to the study. The door of the study was ajar. Derk heard Derrickll on the phone talking to someone. Derk heard Derrickll divulge a shocking plan to steal secrets and destroy the oppositions credibility. Derk waited until Derrickl was free on the phone, Derk made his entrance.

Derrickll, what are you doing? I overheard your telephone conversation. How could you devise such an underhanded, scheme? And especially to those people, who helped us during troubled times. Or have you forgotten? And I thank them, replied Derrickll, but business is business. And you had better not repeat any of this, especially to dad.

I cannot let you do this Derrickll, said Derk. And how are you going to stop me? Go crying to dear old dad? If you do this I will go to the police about Matthias, said Derk. Little Brother said Derrickll, walking over to Derk and violently shoving him up against the wall. If you dare defy me, Said Derrickll, holding a hot poker from the fireplace up to his brothers face. I will destroy you and see to it that you are permanently out of this family for the rest of your life, now is that understood? Said Derrickll. ("Are you going to kill me to? Asked Derk. This has got to stop").

I will do what I have to do, replied Derrickll, as he put the poker closer to his brothers' face and then his eye. Derk nodded, Derk knew what Derrickll was capable of doing. Derk had to handle this another way.

Derrickll yelled at Derk, shoving him towards the door. Now you get out of here and you remember what I said.

THE STRANGER

The stranger got into his car to follow Derk. Derk was going to his law office The stranger watched Derk pull into his private parking space. Derk headed for his office. The stranger watched for about twenty minutes from a distance. He used his binoculars and saw Derk sitting at his desk in his office.

The stranger heard a blast , like a gunshot, and saw flames overcome the area of Derks' office. The stranger ran into the burning building. Derk ,had, been overcome by the smoke and the fumes. The stranger lifted Derk up into his arms and carried Derk outdoors. Laying him down gently on the greenery. The stranger grabbed the office fire extinguisher and went to work, battling the flames.

The stranger grabbed armfuls of files, documents, ledgers, putting them into a spreaded woolen blanket that the stranger had laid on the floor. The stranger confiscated as many documents as he could, grabbing the blanket and fixing it into a bundle. The stranger threw the bundle over his back.

With the flame coming closer and closer to the stranger, he took a rope from his belt, throwing the rope out of the window.The stranger escaped the flames, via the window. The stranger maneuvered to the ground. The stranger saw Derrickll looking up at him. The stranger finally reaching the ground, looked into Derrickll' eyes. Derrickll pulled a daggar from his inside trench coat pocket. Derrickll aimed for the strangers chest. The stranger grabbed Derrickll' one daggar wielding hand, with one arm, the stranger forced Derrickll to drop the daggar. Derrickll turned and ran for his car. Derrickll jumped into his car and sped off.

The stranger walked over to Derk, and gave him CPR; The stranger finally revived Derk. The stranger lifted Derk up in his arms, after blindfolding him. The stranger gently lowered Derk into his car. The stranger went back for Derks' documents, putting them on the seat next to Derk. The stranger delivered Derk to Ebony (his mother). Ebony eas working on her books in their condominium on the other side of town (second home).

The stranger hid in the shadows, watching for Ebony to collect Derk. (The stranger had banged on the door). Finally from the shadows watching, the stranger saw Ebony appear. The stranger watched the two until nothing was visible except for a closed door.

The stranger got into his car and quietly left. Derk would be alright, and his business would be okay, thanks to the stranger. WHO WAS THIS MAN?

REFLECTIONS OF LIFE

DERRICK AND IRENE

Derrickll went to pick up Irene, via a limousine. Of course Irene had to make Derrickll wait twenty minutes. That Irene is always late, complained Derrickll.

The two went to a pop[ular nightspot. Derrickll and Irene had a dinner of succulent seafood. During cocktails, Derrickll disclosed his shocking plan to Irene."Irene said Derrickll, looking into her eyes. MI need a really big favor from you. If all goes right, you and me will be married and live happily, ever after.aid Derrickll, as he pulled out an engagement ring. The ring had a very large diamond. Oh Derrickll, exclaimed Irene, it is beautiful.

Derrickll, put the ring on Irenes' finger. He told Irene that he loved her and wanted to marry her. Before you answer, sweetheart, I have one other problem. You see Derrickll, this has to be taken care of in order for us to be happy and raise a family.

What is that, asked Irene? Phillips Industries, replied Derrickll. All you have to do is apply for a job, and once you are hired, you take this beautiful ring and take all the pictures of how the plant operates. As many pictures as you can. Pictures of trap doors, everything, said Derrickll. "Derrickll, replied Irene, you are asking me to betray my friends".

Okay, said Derrickll, if you won't help me, I will just have to find someone else who will. Derrickll stood up to leave. Irene was weak for Derrickll. Irene got up, and ran behind Derrickll. Derrickll wait, said Irene,

As she reached inside, Derrickll' inside pocket, taking out the ring., She started putting the ring on her finger. Irene and Derrickll stayed the night together at the cabin.

Irene knew that Derrickll did not love her, or anyone else for that matter. Since they were kids Irene had always covered for Derrickll.

Irene remembered a time at a school outing. Three classes went to an amusement park, in grammar school. Irene remember that nightmarish roller-coaster ride. Derrickll had an argument with one of the classmates The argument was about who would sit in front. The friend was much bigger than Derrickll. Irene remember Derrickll shoving the boy out of the roller-coaster, while the ride was still in motion.

The classmates fall was broken, by a circus tent. The classmate did live, but he sustained multiple fractures. He never remembered the incident. I guess since that time, Irene and Derrickll had a bond.

Something unexplainable kept pulling Irene in Derrickll' direction. Irene did not know what it was. Some strange force had hold of Irene, and she could not seem to break the tie. POOR IRENE, IRENE DOESN'T RECOGNIZE SATAN IN HER PRESENCE. IRENE MUST BREAK AWAY OR SHE IS HEADED FOR SELF DESTRUCTION.

KATHERINE, KATY, BRADLEY

Little Katy hurriedly answered the phone. Her mother Katherine was at a ribbon- cutting event. Katherine was having the grand opening of her third catering business. Katherines' catering business was special., each business catered to different ethnic groups, there were three subdivisions.

Katherine headed the parent division or the American cuisine. The other three subdivisions were; Afro American, Hispanic, and the final division was Indian cuisine. Katherine would continue to expand once the others began to run smoothly. Katherine had to get a clientele and a good advertising executive. Expansions would come in time. There were many countries and many different types of food.

Hello said Little Katy as she answered the phone. There was a long silence on the other end of the line. Little Katy was now sixteen years old and Little Katy wasn't so little anymore. I guess Little Katys' nickname stuck with her throughout the years.

Hello, said a deep voice on the other end of the phone. Pick the package up at point B; deliver the package to point D. There awaits your client. Point A, meant the house across from the park, where Katy would pick up the top secret information. Point D was the motel on the edge of town room number 250.

The call girl ring had been operating in the town for about two months. The workers were paid a percentage. Most of the young people hung out at the sweets shop, where teenagers gathered. The secret information, consisted of powerful political figures who catered to the young kids. Little Katy was among this crowd.

All the kids knew, was that a man came into town once a week to pay for information gathered. Since the mans identity was unknown, the call girl ring was allowed to go on. For a fee.

Little Katy had acquired a new car and clothes, and yet, no one suspected a thing, since these things were kept secretly. The criminal element assisted Little Katy in storing her car. Little Katy loved school.

Little Katy exchanged sexual favors for money. Little Katy accepted information, which she turned over to someone else.for money who is this predator? He is a student, and this is how he is paying his way through college.

His name is twenty four year old Glen Stamford. Son of Anna and Jerrod Stamford. Jerrod and Anna have refused him his entertainment expenses, and the use of his sports car. For two semesters. Glen had to bring up his grade point average. Now Glen is using the internet to conduct illigeal business practices.

No one knew that Glenn was the actual head of this wrongful business practice. The man that went to town once a week was not Glenn. The man worked for Glenn. No one knew Glenns' identity. Glenn was a master of disguises. Glenns' secret life was about to be rudely interrupted.

You see Glenn bragged about it casually to Allan one day. What happens when Allan finds out that Cecilia was a call-girl. Cil was secretly working for Glenn. You see this practice has made Glenn a millionaire, Jerrod and Anna were in for a big surprise.

DAVID SR. AND MATTHEW

What are you so nervous about, asked David Sr? As he helped Mathew with his tie. I don't know dad, said Matthew. I have been dating Helena for almost six months, and sitting next to her parents at Helenas' dance recitals. It still makes me nervous.

Matthew, said David Sr. just be yourself, and Helenas' parents can't help but love you. I pray that you are right, said Matthew. Helena was a dancer. Matthew and Helena had been dating for six months. Helenas' parents owned and operated the family inn. Helena was twenty-two years old; Matthew was finishing his last year of college,and managed the family business in Texas. Matthew was in and out of town a lot. Matthew enjoyed playing basketball. Matthew had hoped to be a professional athlete. Because of the family business, Matthew put that part of his life on hold.

LIVES IN JEOPARDY

Menna and David Sr. and their children had moved into the mansion. David Sr. mother who was getting on in years, now occupied the mansion. David Sr, did not want his mother to live in that big place alone. Mrs. Phillips, stayed in the mansion. I guess it made her feel closer to her deceased husband and held a lot of memories.

Aren't you forgetting something Matthew, asked Menna?

Matthew turned and looked back as Menna handed Matthew a corsage. Matthew had sent three dozen roses to Helenas' dressing room, ahead of time. Matthew had to have Helena to the recital hall by 6:30; The curtain would go up at 8:00p.m. Matthew took the family limo, since he could send Gus, (the limo driver); to recover Helenas' parents' by 7:15 p.m.

Helena was patiently waiting for Matthew, when he arrived. Matthew went to the door to help Helena with her costumes. Helena and Matthew arrived to Helenas' dressing room on time. Matthew gently stroked Helenas' cheek and wished her well. Helena thanked Matthew for the lovely flowers. Matthew had the limo driver to take him to the home business office. Matthew had to recover the receipts. Matthew instructed the limo driver to pick up Helenas' parents and stop back for him afterwards. Matthew reminded Gus, the ballet was the Nutcracker.

Matthew watched Helenas' swan-like movements, so graceful. Matthew sat in stone silence, watching the ballet, with Helenas' parents sitting on each side of him. Matthew loosened his tie. Matthew was truly nervous. Parents just make you feel that way. Any person with respect for their elders would feel that way.

By ten o' clock the show was over. Matthew and Helena had planned to enjoy a late dinner after Helenas' parents were returned home. Helenas' parents got out of the limo, Matthew breathed a sigh of relief. Helena giggled. What's' so funny, asked Matthew? Well Matthew dear heart, I could not help but notice how nervous you are with my parents. Try and relax a little more. My parents don't talk much, but they love you Matthew. Please try and remember that.

I suppose you are right, replied Matthew. I guess it is just a reaction. "Well, what do you feel like tonight, asked Helena"? How about French cuisine, said Matthew. Sounds lovely, replied Helena.

By twelve midnight, the couple headed home. Matthew and Helena embraced at the door. Helena reminded Matthew of their quality time, that they would be spending at the lake. With the two always so busy and on the go, they needed to spend sometime away, alone together. Matthew planned to marry Helena someday.

Matthews' drive home, via limo, was a quiet peaceful ride. As the limo turned the corner, Matthew noticed Little Bradley, he was running through a gas station. Matthew motioned for the driver to pull over. Matthew jumped from the car calling Little Bradley.

TO BE CONTINUED...

Please be sure to read Reflections of Life, "Lives in Jeopardy." See what unfolds.

Reflections of Life